Canadian Sports Sites for Kids

Christopher MacKinnon

CANADIAN SPORTS SITES FOR KIDS

Places Named for Speedsters, Scorers, and Other Sportsworld Citizens

DUNDURN
TORONTO

Editor: Allison Hirst
Design: Courtney Horner
Printer: Webcom

All illustrations by Matt McInnes

Library and Archives Canada Cataloguing in Publication

MacKinnon, Christopher, 1978-

    Canadian sports sites for kids : places named for speedsters, scorers, and other sportsworld citizens / by Christopher MacKinnon.

Issued also in electronic format.
ISBN 978-1-4597-0705-4

    1. Names, Geographical--Canada--Juvenile literature. 2. Sports--Miscellanea--Juvenile literature. I. Title.

FC36.M23 2012   j917.1'0014   C2012-904615-9

1 2 3 4 5   16 15 14 13 12

We acknowledge the support of the **Canada Council for the Arts** and the **Ontario Arts Council** for our publishing program. We also acknowledge the financial support of the **Government of Canada** through the **Canada Book Fund** and **Livres Canada Books**, and the **Government of Ontario** through the **Ontario Book Publishing Tax Credit** and the **Ontario Media Development Corporation**.

Care has been taken to trace the ownership of copyright material used in this book. The author and the publisher welcome any information enabling them to rectify any references or credits in subsequent editions.

J. Kirk Howard, President

Printed and bound in Canada.
www.dundurn.com

Visit us at
Dundurn.com
Definingcanada.ca
@dundurnpress
Facebook.com/dundurnpress

Dundurn	Gazelle Book Services Limited	Dundurn
3 Church Street, Suite 500	White Cross Mills	2250 Military Road
Toronto, Ontario, Canada	High Town, Lancaster, England	Tonawanda, NY
M5E 1M2	LA1 4XS	U.S.A. 14150

DISCARDED

For Aidan and George

Acknowledgements

I would like to give a special nod to illustrator Matt McInnes, whose imaginative maps and drawings of Canada's sports geography are a key contribution to this book.

Many thanks as well to Colleen MacKinnon and Mark McInnes of St. Catharines, Ontario, who provided encouragement and early feedback on the manuscript. Thanks also to Jordon Vinette of the Planning, Property and Development Department at the City of Winnipeg for putting me in touch with Mr. Liggins. Athletic geographers Francis Treblesmith, Leslie Gaines, and Brenda Stairs took an early interest in the book. I thank them for their support and insightful comments. Sporting landscapers Lisa Jaynes, Thomas Grocer, and Joel Stackhouse also provided useful advice and game plan ideas along the way.

Introduction

Canadians are curious about place names. Especially the odd-sounding ones like Head-Smashed-In Buffalo Jump (Saskatchewan) and Punkeydoodles Corners (Ontario). There's even an entire branch of our national government dedicated to cataloguing every place name in Canada.

But towns, rivers, and mountains aren't the only features that need names. Parks, streets, and buildings require them, too. And since we Canadians love our sports, we've named lots of these places after stars from the sports world. Many athletes who have won trophies and prizes say their proudest moment wasn't when they scored an important goal or made a game-winning catch, it was when a street or school was named in their honour. In Canada, sports isn't just entertainment; it's literally part of the landscape.

I started counting "player place names" as a kid growing up in Ontario. I lived near the hometown of Wayne Gretzky, the greatest scorer in NHL history, and I remember often seeing the big green sign on the road pointing to a place called Wayne Gretzky Parkway. I've since added more than 250 places to my list and, all these years later, I'm still counting.

Number 99

Wayne Gretzky, the greatest goal-scorer in NHL history, is often referred to simply as "Number 99." Gretzky wore number 99 on his jersey his entire career and a story circulates to this day that his original contract with the Oilers was for an incredible 99 years. The Ontario Hockey League even has a trophy called the Wayne Gretzky 99 Award, given each year to the league's playoff MVP. So in what year did the city of Edmonton decide to rename one of its major streets **Wayne Gretzky Drive**? In 1999, of course.

Fore!

On April 13, 2004, the mayor of Sarnia held a special outdoor ceremony to officially name a city park in honour of champion Canadian golfer Mike Weir. The site for **Mike Weir Park** was chosen because it's where Mike practised hitting golf balls as a kid – even though he knew it was against the law.

At the ceremony that day, the assembled crowd chuckled as mayor Mike Bradley presented Weir with a sign formerly posted at the park. It read: HITTING OF GOLF BALLS PROHIBITED. BY-LAW #7867.

"The Longest Gold Medal Race in History"

By kindergarten, every kid knows that cheating is wrong. Too bad some grownup athletes sometimes forget that simple lesson. At the 2002 Olympic Winter Games in Salt Lake City, two Russian skiers learned their lesson the hard way.

On February 15, Canadians had watched with pride as Beckie Scott of Alberta – already the namesake of the **Beckie Scott Nordic Centre** in Invermere, British Columbia – won a hard-fought bronze medal in the women's five-kilometre pursuit. A couple of amazingly fast skiers from Russia took the gold and silver medals.

But just days later, the International Olympic Committee (IOC) revealed to the world that the two skiers who'd finished ahead of Scott had tested positive for a performance-enhancing drug called darbepoetin. That's against the rules, the Canadian Olympic Committee (COC) pointed out. The IOC agreed – two years and four months later! With the Russians now disqualified, a patient Beckie Scott was upgraded to the gold medal she deserved.

Hundreds of people came out to the Vancouver Art Gallery on June 24, 2004, to see Beckie Scott finally receive her gold medal. "It may be the longest gold medal race in history, but we won and we are thrilled to present Beckie with her well-deserved and long overdue gold medal," said COC president Michael Chambers.

Two years later, Scott won a silver medal with teammate Sara Renner in the team sprint event at the 2006 Olympics in Turin.

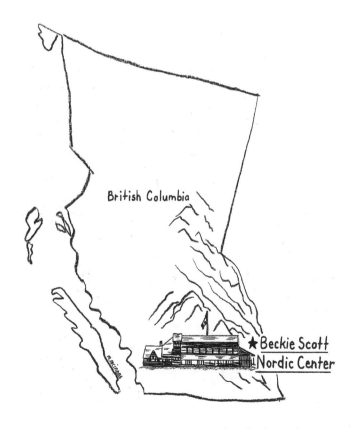

British Columbia

★ Beckie Scott
Nordic Center

Pedal to the Metal

Canadian race car driver Greg Moore was part of one of the most dramatic Indy Car race finishes ever. Going into the final lap of the Detroit Indy Grand Prix on June 8, 1997, Moore seemed certain to finish no better than third place. He had driven well that day, but leader Mauricio Gugelmin and second-place driver Mark Blundell were comfortably ahead with the finish line almost in sight. No one expected what happened next. In the final stretch, Gugelmin, instead of cruising to victory, ran out of fuel. This allowed his teammate, Blundell, to take the lead. Incredibly, Blundell also ran out of gas moments later. They could only watch helplessly as the Canadian took full advantage, zipping into first place for the win. The exasperated television announcer could hardly believe his eyes, shouting, "Is it possible that first and second place run out of fuel on the last lap!!!"

Sadly, Moore died in a racing accident in California on Halloween 1999. But folks in British Columbia have kept his memory alive with the **Greg Moore Youth Centre**, a popular recreation centre that was opened in Maple Ridge in 2003. The centre is for teens aged 13–18 and features areas for basketball, floor hockey, skateboarding, rock climbing, and indoor soccer.

Hometown Hockey Hero

Two of the three NHL teams Mario Gosselin (1963–) played for — the Hartford Whalers and the Quebec Nordiques — no longer exist. A goalie who played 12 NHL seasons, Gosselin achieved 20 wins in 1988, a career high.

HOMETOWN TRIBUTE

Aréna Mario-Gosselin, Thetford Mines, Quebec.

Sports Pages

Canadian golfer Mike Weir, who has a park named after him in Sarnia and a street named after him in Utah, is also an author. In 2001, Weir published *On Course with Mike Weir: Insights and Instructions from a Left-Hander on the PGA Tour*. The book is co-written with sportswriters Tim Campbell and Scott Morrison.

Politics Is a Contact Sport

Politics is often compared to a contact sport. But from 1982 to 1992, the people of Alberta took this adage literally. During these years, both of their premiers, the province's political leader, were former Edmonton Eskimos football players!

Peter Lougheed was elected premier of Alberta in 1982. He only played in the CFL for two years, as a defensive end from 1949 to 1950. Alberta's **Peter Lougheed Provincial Park** is named after him. A hospital in Calgary, the **Peter Lougheed Centre**, also bears his name.

Don Getty, premier from 1985 to 1992, was a star quarterback for the Eskimos for ten years. He still ranks third all-time in passing yards for Canadian quarterbacks and he won the Grey Cup with the Eskimos twice. **Don Getty Provincial Wildlands Park** near Kananaskis, Alberta, was named for him in 2001.

The Luck of St. Patrick

Billy Sherring was a poorly paid brakeman for the Grand Trunk Railway when he was chosen to represent Canada at the 1906 Olympic Games in Athens, Greece. Back then, athletes had to pay their own way to international events, so it seemed there was no way Billy could make the long journey. But Billy's friends were determined to see him compete for Canada.

According to stories, fellow athletes at the St. Patrick's Athletic Club in Hamilton – the club's emblem was a huge shamrock – collected cash donations and then bet the entire amount on a racehorse called *Cicely*. The lucky horse won at 20 to 1 odds and Billy was soon on a steamer bound for the land of Zeus and Socrates.

Billy won a gold medal in marathon at the Games. **Billy Sherring Park** in Hamilton now stands as a reminder of a remarkable achievement, which without a little luck might never have happened.

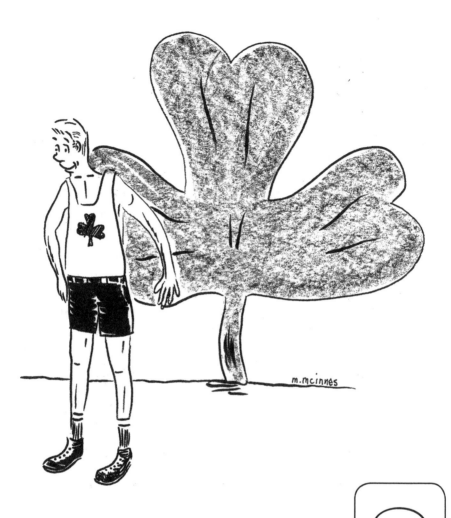

Did You Know?

The Sault Sabercats of the Ontario Varsity Football League play their home games at **Rocky DiPietro Field**. DiPietro played his entire 14-year CFL career with the Hamilton Tiger-Cats. The wide receiver, born in Sault Ste. Marie in 1956, scored 45 career touchdowns as a Tiger Cat and became the Canadian Football League's all-time pass reception leader in 1989. He was inducted into the CFL Hall of Fame in 1997.

"Daredevil Downey"

Clarence Downey, who was nicknamed "Daredevil Downey," dazzled Saskatchewan crowds during the Great Depression with his amazing barrel-jumping feats. Travelling on ice skates at nearly 50 kilometres an hour, Downey would dart through flaming hoops before launching himself over long rows of barrels stacked end to end.

The sport of barrel-jumping – long jumping on ice skates – grew out of speed skating and became very popular during the 1920s and 1930s. In 1936, Daredevil Downey won the Saskatchewan barrel-jumping championships and from 1937 to 1940 he was the barrel-jumping champion of Western Canada. To recognize these and Downey's other speed skating exploits, Saskatoon named the **Clarence Downey Speed Skating Oval** after him in February 1971.

Her Excellency's Cup

Lord Frederick Arthur Stanley, who served as governor general of Canada from 1888 to 1893, was the original donor of the

National Hockey League's Stanley Cup. On March 18, 1892, he announced he was going to donate the championship trophy to the league – and the rest is history.

Like the Stanley Cup, the Clarkson Cup of women's hockey was also created by and named after a governor general. On September 14, 2005, Her Excellency the Right Honourable Governor General Adrienne Clarkson announced she was donating a new championship trophy for the top women's hockey club in Canada. The Clarkson Cup was first won in 2009 by the Montreal Stars.

The creation of the Clarkson Cup happened just a year after the naming of **Adrienne Clarkson Public School** in Richmond Hill, Ontario, and two years after the naming of **Adrienne Clarkson Elementary School** in Nepean, Ontario.

Clare's Bears

Clare Drake coached briefly with the Winnipeg Jets of the NHL and the Edmonton Eskimos of the CFL, but he is best remembered for his record-setting career with the University of Alberta (U of A) Golden Bears.

Over 28 years he won 697 games as coach of the Golden Bears hockey team. That's more than any other coach in the history of world university sports. The year 1968 in particular was a big one for Clare. That year, he coached the U of A football *and* hockey teams to national titles, becoming the only person ever to coach national champions in two sports in the same year. On June 1, 1990, the University of Alberta announced that from that day forward Varsity Arena, the university's 3,000-seat hockey rink, would be called **Clare Drake Arena**.

Solid Circuitry

The **Circuit Gilles Villeneuve** is one of Canada's elite motor racing tracks. It's built on a man-made island in the St. Lawrence River at Montreal and is the venue for Formula One, NASCAR, and Grand-Am Rolex Sports Car Series races.

The track used to be called the Île Notre-Dame Circuit, but was renamed in honour of legendary Canadian Formula One driver Gilles Villeneuve following his death in 1982. Villeneuve won six Grand Prix races between 1977 and 1982. The circuit is one of two Canadian places named for Villeneuve. **Parc Gilles-Villeneuve**, dedicated in 1988, can be found in the town of Berthierville, Quebec, where the racing legend grew up.

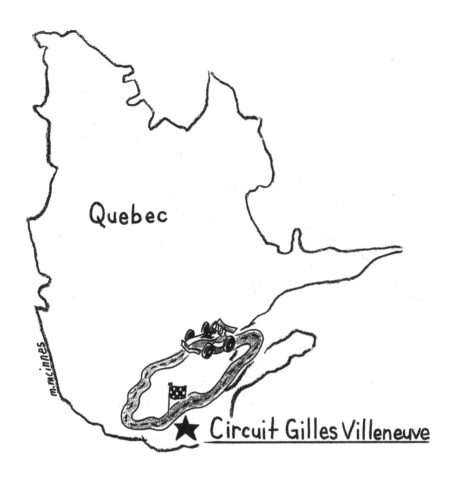

Quebec

m.mcinnes

★ Circuit Gilles Villeneuve

Captain Video

A brilliant and eccentric coach known for fresh ideas, Roger Nielson was the first to use videotape to analyze other teams and his own. That's how he got one of the best nicknames in hockey history, "Captain Video." His preference for "colourfully blinding ties" was also pointed out by the hockey writer Stan Fischler. In all, Neilson coached eight NHL teams, including the Toronto Maple Leafs, Vancouver Canucks, New York Rangers, and Ottawa Senators.

Since Captain Video passed away in 2003, tributes in his honour have deservedly piled up. Not surprisingly, two of these

– **Roger Neilson Public School** and **Roger Neilson Way** –
are located in the city of Peterborough, Ontario, where Neilson
coached the OHL's Peterborough Petes for ten years. Go east
a few kilometres and you'll find two more: Ottawa is not only
home to **Roger's House**, a facility for sick kids at the Children's
Hospital of Eastern Ontario, but it's also the whereabouts of **The
Roger Neilson Room**, a special chamber within Scotiabank
Place where coaches of the Ottawa Senators meet to plan
strategy. In this room, many lieutenants have gathered, but there
will never be another Captain.

Slugger Seaman

Major-leaguer Phil "Babe" Marchildon of the old Philadelphia
Athletics once said that Dannie Seaman "hits the ball too hard
and too often to be playing in Nova Scotia." But Seaman never
made it to the big leagues despite a nearly .300 batting average
over several seasons with the Liverpool Larrupers, an unofficial
farm club of the Boston Red Sox.

After his playing days were over, Seaman coached amateur
teams. Tragically, he died while refereeing a college basketball
game in 1973. A written tribute to Dannie Seaman can be found
today on a plaque decorating a stone monument in **Dannie
Seaman Park** in Liverpool, Nova Scotia.

Defenceman Turned GG

When the Harvard Crimson men's ice hockey team defeated
Boston College 4–3 in overtime one winter evening in 1963 to
win the Cleary Cup, the players could hardly have known that
one of their teammates would one day become the highest-
ranking official in Canada.

David Johnston, who was installed as Canada's governor
general in October of 2010, was a star defenceman for that

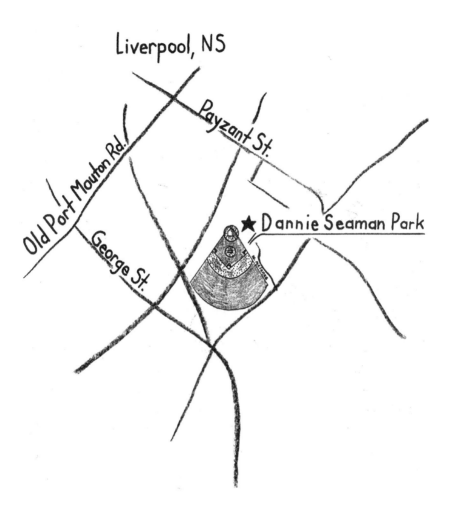

Liverpool, NS

Old Port Mouton Rd.

Payzant St.

George St.

★ Dannie Seaman Park

victorious Harvard Crimson team – in fact, he was the team captain. In 1962 and 1963, Johnston had also been named to the Ivy League Men's Ice Hockey All-American team.

On June 5, 2011, true sports buffs were likely harkening back to Johnston's days patrolling blue lines for the Crimson. That day, the University of Waterloo (UW) community officially unveiled the newly named **David Johnston Research + Technology Park** on campus – a tribute to Johnston's role as former UW president and his new post as governor general, you understand, hockey credentials notwithstanding.

If you pass by the park, you'll notice the plus symbol placed between the words *research* and *technology* on all signage. The university decided to go with the more unusual plus sign instead of the customary ampersand or the word *and*.

Boxing Boulevard

Halifax's **Buddy Daye Street**, named in 2003, may be the only road in Canada named for a boxing champion. Delmore Daye, who the Nova Scotia Sports Hall of Fame says was "better known in the fistic world as Buddy Daye," compiled a record of 81 wins and only six losses during his career. From 1964 to 1966, he held the title of Canadian junior lightweight boxing champion.

Long after Daye's last appearance in the ring, his years of community involvement earned him a different kind of honour. He was made the sergeant-at-arms of the Nova Scotia legislature in 1990.

According to the Nova Scotia government, Daye was "the first African Nova Scotian" appointed to the sergeant-at-arms role. Another honour for the late pugilist followed in 2012. In May, the Nova Scotia Department of Education announced it was spending more than $2 million to build the **Delmore "Buddy" Daye Africentric Learning Institute**, to "provide more support and resources for students of African descent." Will the new school's sports teams be called "the Boxers"?

Hockey School

In Parry Sound, Ontario, where Bobby Orr was born and raised, two buildings have been named for him. In Boston, where he spent most of his amazing Hall of Fame career with the Boston Bruins, there's a big statue of him on a street called Legends Way. But how did a school in Oshawa, Ontario, come to be named **Bobby Orr Public School**?

Between the ages of 14 to 18, Orr lived in Oshawa and played for the Oshawa Generals of the OHA before moving up to the NHL. He was an all-star three of his four seasons with the Generals and he set a record for goals by a defenceman – a record that still stands today. His number 2 sweater was also retired by the team in 2008 (he wore number 4 throughout his NHL career).

On September 8, 2004, the first day of classes at the new Bobby Orr Public School, the former Oshawa General spoke to the 320 students who gathered for an assembly. "I've been a lucky person," Orr told the students, who gave him two standing ovations. "Over the years I've received a couple of awards. But having my name put on a school tops them all."

The Athlete Who Could Do Everything

Sandwiched between the CN Tower and the Rogers Centre in downtown Toronto is a small patch of green space called **Bobbie Rosenfeld Park**. A one-time chocolate factory worker, Fanny "Bobbie" Rosenfeld became one of the best multi-sport athletes in Canadian history. In 1949, the Canadian Press named her "Canada's Female Athlete of the Half-Century" with good reason. Rosenfeld won two silver medals at the 1928 Olympics in Amsterdam, pioneered women's hockey, was a Toronto tennis champion, and also won titles in discus, shot put, and softball. A biography of Rosenfeld by writer Anne Dublin is aptly called *Bobbie Rosenfeld: The Athlete Who Could Do Everything*.

Sherring's Missing Gold

Billy Sherring brought great honour to his hometown of Hamilton, Ontario, when he won the gold medal in marathon at the 1906 Olympic Games in Athens. Prince George II of Greece even ran the final stretch of the race alongside him. Hamilton still displays its pride in the famous runner with **Billy Sherring Park** and an annual memorial race named in his honour.

But some Olympic record books don't even mention Billy Sherring's greatest win. Did Billy's gold medal really count?

It certainly did at the time. But the 1906 Olympics are something of a historical oddity. St. Louis had hosted the Games in 1904, and Rome was to hold them in 1908. So from our modern viewpoint, there never was supposed to be an Olympics in 1906. Indeed, this turned out to be the only time such a "monkey in the middle" Olympics was ever held. The IOC eventually took the step of downgrading the 1906 Olympics to unofficial status, thereby demoting all the medals that were won that summer in Greece. Put it this way: we all know Billy's medal is real; it's just not "official" in the strictest sense of the word.

Foreign Affairs

The University of Kansas in Lawrence, Kansas, is the place hoops fanatics need to visit to pay homage to Dr. James Naismith, the Canadian who invented basketball. And what is the university's claim to fame? Naismith taught and coached for decades at the school. Pay a visit to the historic Phog Allen Fieldhouse ("The Phog"), where the **James Naismith Court** is the home hardwood for the school's basketball team, the Jayhawks. Not coincidentally, it's located on a street called **Naismith Drive**. Nearby **Naismith Hall** is one of the campus's student residences.

Did You Know?

James Naismith, the inventor of basketball, was a standout football player as a student at McGill University in the 1880s. He played two seasons for the team now known as the McGill Redmen and was awarded McGill's prestigious Wickstead Athletic Medal in 1887. Two eastern Ontario streets are named after him, **James Naismith Way** in Almonte and **James Naismith Drive** in Ottawa.

The Flying Father

With two playoff goals and four points, left winger Les Costello helped the Toronto Maple Leafs win the Stanley Cup in 1948. He played for the Leafs in each of the following two seasons, but then he made an unusual career change.

Costello retired from professional hockey and studied to become a Catholic priest. He was then assigned to lead the parish of St. Alphonsus Church in his hometown of Timmins, Ontario. Costello still loved hockey, though, and he soon became a well-known figure throughout Canada as his all-priest hockey team, The Flying Fathers, toured the country raising millions of dollars for charity.

In September of 2003, the city of Timmins renamed First Avenue **Father Costello Drive**. Cobalt, Ontario, also paid a tribute to the hockey playing priest that year with the naming of **Father Les Costello Memorial Arena**.

Mr. Speaker

After three exhibition games with the NFL's Green Bay Packers in 1956, Louisiana-born Emery Barnes came to Canada in his late twenties hoping to catch on with a team in the Canadian Football League.

When a leg injury kept Barnes off the field, he began studying the politics of his new country instead. His studies certainly paid off. In 1972, he was elected to the British Columbia legislature and later he made history as the first black Speaker in any province. Barnes did return to football, playing 30 career games for the BC Lions, but it's his political achievements that are most remembered. **Emery Barnes Park** in Vancouver's Yaletown area was named for him on September 27, 2003.

Foreign Affairs

Every day, aspiring young athletes exercise their lats, deltoids, biceps and triceps in the **Harry Jerome Weight Room** at the University of Oregon (U of O). Born in Prince Albert, Saskatchewan, Harry Jerome competed for Canada in three Olympics, winning a bronze medal at the 1964 Games in Tokyo. He attended the University of Oregon in the city of Eugene in the early 1960s. At the U of O, Jerome is still venerated as "the most accomplished track and field athlete" in the school's history.

Row, Row, Row Your Boat

On October 1, 2006, the University of British Columbia (UBC) officially opened the **John M.S. Lecky Boathouse** as the new home of the UBC Thunderbirds renowned rowing program. The boathouse, located in Richmond, B.C., is named after John MacMillan Stirling Lecky, who won a silver medal in rowing for Canada at the 1960 Olympics in Rome. The highlight of his career came in 1964 when he won Canada's oldest and most prestigious rowing event, the Royal Canadian Henley Regatta.

Interestingly, Lecky wasn't the first former Henley winner to get a building named in his honour. There has been a **Hilton Belyea Arena** in Saint John, New Brunswick, since 1974. Belyea, who was also a champion speed skater, won the Henley in 1921 and 1922.

Hoops

Robert Gordon, born in 1940, has carved out a distinguished career in the fields of education and post-secondary administration. He holds degrees from several universities, including Harvard. Perhaps these are the reasons Toronto's Humber College named its **Robert A. Gordon Learning Centre** after him.

But Gordon's basketball days should be considered, as well. His Bishop's University Wall of Distinction biography says he "ruled the basketball world at Bishop's in the early '60s" and states that his "keen shooting touch and aggressive drives to the basket made him the leading scorer in the OSLAA in the 1962–1963 season."

Haunted Happenings

Late one night, two students decide to explore the underground tunnels that connect the buildings on their college campus. After poking around some empty rooms, they hear what sounds like someone whistling. They turn in the direction of the sound, but nothing is seen and the noise abruptly stops. Before leaving the tunnels, the students again hear the eerie singsong notes, then they're hit by a frigid burst of wind that seems to come from … well, nowhere.

A construction worker doing some after-hours repairs in a dim passageway sees a woman walk past him. He finds this odd since it is late at night and no one else is supposed to be around. He notices she is wearing a nurse's outfit. He calls out, but she rounds a corner and disappears. He feels compelled to follow and when he finally catches up, the woman slowly turns around and faces him. She has no face and only a featureless void where one should be.

These are just a couple of the many ghost stories that have been reported around the **Robert A. Gordon Learning Centre**, named after the leading player in Bishop's University basketball history and part of the Humber College Lakeshore Campus in Toronto. The solid, recently renovated buildings on the campus may look modern enough, but they were built way back in 1888. For most of their history, these buildings were a kind of hospital for mentally ill patients known as the Mimico Insane Asylum.

Since Humber moved in, countless reports of spooky, unexplained happenings have brought the campus a reputation as one of the most haunted places in Canada. Skeptics dismiss most of these reports as nonsense, though, and the Internet buzzes with sites both promoting and debunking the "evidence."

"Mom, Dad, I'm an Orphan"

Former Toronto Maple Leafs goalie Harry Lumley – namesake of the **Harry Lumley Bayshore Community Centre** in Owen Sound, Ontario – played one season in the 1940s for a team called the Owen Sound Orphans. Team members, all teenagers, hadn't lost their parents, though. The team was called the Orphans because it couldn't find a sponsor.

Harmsworth Winner

The prestigious Harmsworth Trophy, also known as the British International Trophy for Motorboats, was commissioned in 1903 by Viscount Charles Harmsworth of England. Bob Hayward, who grew up on a chicken farm in Embro, Ontario, is the only Canadian ever to win it.

In 1961, Hayward was piloting his speedboat in another race, the Silver Cup Regatta on the Detroit River, when tragedy struck. His boat flipped while travelling more than 280 kilometres per hour and the impact of the crash claimed the 33-year-old's life. Despite the shortness of his career, his surprising Harmsworth victories in 1959, 1960, and 1961 make him a key figure in powerboating history. The **Bob Hayward YMCA** in London, Ontario, was named for him in 1963.

The **Hayward Long Reach** in Ontario's Prince Edward County is also named for Bob Hayward. Like a skinny aquatic arm, it's a long and narrow section of water that "reaches" southward from the town of Deseronto toward Picton. The level, straight nautical setting is perfect for powerboat races and it's where several of Bob's biggest contests took place as crowds of spectators looked on from the shoreline. Although locals have called it the Hayward Long Reach since the 1960s, the place name only became official in 2011, the same year Canada Post issued a special stamp depicting Hayward and his famous boat, *Miss Supertest III*.

Hometown Hockey Hero

Jean Béliveau (1931–) played his entire career with the Montreal Canadiens, winning ten Stanley Cups. A member of the Hockey Hall of Fame, Béliveau recorded 507 goals and 712 assists in 1,125 NHL games.

HOMETOWN TRIBUTE:

Pavillon Jean-Béliveau, Victoriaville, Quebec.

An Aquatic Allan

In 1940, a young swimmer from Peterborough, Ontario, named Allan Marshall swam a time of 2:33:20 in the 200-yard breaststroke at the Summer National Championship in Verdun, Quebec. It was a new Canadian record. Incredibly, Marshall would end up holding five separate Canadian swimming records in his short career. Today, the **Allan Marshall Pool** is the main swimming facility at Trent University in Peterborough.

Swimming Into the Record Books

George Vernot Park in Montreal's inner city stands as a quiet reminder of a unique Canadian sports fact. In 1920, a 19-year-old French Canadian named George Vernot travelled to Antwerp, Belgium, to compete for Canada at the Olympics. The young swimmer won a silver medal in the 1,500-metre freestyle event. Incredibly, after more than nine decades, Vernot remains the

Hometown Hockey Hero

Babe Siebert (1904–39) was named the new head coach of the Montreal Canadiens before the start of the 1939 season. But that summer Siebert drowned at his family resort on Lake Huron. "Swimming out to get an inflatable tire that his children had been playing with," says a biography on the Legends of Hockey website, Siebert "apparently grew fatigued and simply disappeared from sight."

HOMETOWN TRIBUTE:

Babe Siebert Memorial Arena, Zurich, Ontario.

only Canadian to ever win an Olympic medal in that event! Also in Antwerp, Vernot earned a bronze in the 400-metre freestyle. Only two other Canadians have ever medalled in that event.

Strong-Arm Tactics

It's often said that when life gives you lemons, you make lemonade. So what did Fred Salvador do when a serious leg injury slammed the door on his football dreams with the Montreal Alouettes? He discovered a sport that required only upper body strength: arm wrestling.

Salvador's citation at the Canadian Arm Wrestling Federation Hall of Fame says he was born and raised in Timmins, Ontario, and organized the first ever Canadian Arm Wrestling Championships in 1971. It was a stroke of brilliance when he managed to convince the U.S. producers of the hit television show *Wide*

World of Sports to send a team up to northern Ontario to cover his arm wrestling events. The sport had never known that level of exposure. Supervised by Salvador, the World Armwrestling Championships took place 12 years in a row in Timmins.

As a tribute, the city of Timmins officially unveiled the **Fred Salvador Athletic Field** in August of 2007.

Trading Names

Sometimes it's easier to give a new name to a place that already exists, rather than build something entirely new. Here's a look at what some buildings, parks, and streets used to be called.

Current Name	Former Name
Wayne Gretzky Drive	Capilano Drive (Edmonton)
Cindy Klassen Way	Recreation Road (Winnipeg)
Mike Weir Park	Huronview Park (Sarnia)
John Tonelli Arena	Community Sports Complex (Milton, Ontario)
Circuit Gilles Villeneuve	Île Notre Dame Circuit (Montreal)
Elvis Stojko Arena	Observatory Arena (Richmond Hill, Ontario)
Milt Stegall Drive	Arena Road (Winnipeg)
Ivor Wynne Stadium	Civic Stadium (Hamilton)
Susan Auch Park	Triangle Park (Winnipeg)
Nat Bailey Stadium	Capilano Stadium (Vancouver)
Marilyn Bell Park	Sunnyside Waterfront (Toronto)
Buddy Daye Street	Gerrish Street (Halifax)
Charmaine Hooper Soccer Fields	Colonnade Soccer Fields (Nepean, Ontario)
Bill Hunter Arena	Jasper Place Arena (Edmonton)
Bill Mosienko Arena	Keewatin Arena (Winnipeg)
Aréna Roberto Luongo	Aréna Hebert (Montreal)

Special Fan

It's no surprise that folks in lots of Canadian towns and cities have named places after hockey players, hockey coaches, and even hockey team owners. But a hockey *fan*? It happened in March 2011, in Burford, Ontario.

In late 2010, a woman known locally simply as "Mary" passed away after decades of cheering for the Burford Bulldogs of the Southern Ontario Junior Hockey League. According to reports, she was a "vociferous" hockey fan that liked to crochet as she kept score. Mary would loudly harangue any referee who dared make a call against her beloved Bulldogs. Some say her voice still haunts the arena on game nights.

Today her name lives on. In a special ceremony in March of 2011, which was attended by family, friends, and dignitaries, the new **Mary Lowes Community Room** was officially opened on the first floor of the Burford Arena, the Bulldogs' home rink.

Hometown Hockey Hero

New Jersey Devils goaltender Martin Brodeur (1972–) is one of the best goalies of all-time. With a win against the Chicago Blackhawks on St. Patrick's Day in 2009, Brodeur became the all-time leader in wins by a goalie with 552.

HOMETOWN TRIBUTE:

Aréna Martin-Brodeur, Saint-Léonard, Montreal, Quebec.

Two Arénas

Was Leonard the patron saint of goalies? In St-Léonard, one of the 19 boroughs of Montreal, both arenas are named after all-star NHL netminders who grew up in the neighbourhood. The two buildings are less than a five-minute drive from each other. **Aréna Roberto Luongo**, at 5300 Boulevard Robert, was named at a special ceremony attended by the Canucks' goalie on August 22, 2009. Over at 7755 Rue Colbert, you'll find **Aréna Martin Brodeur**, a tribute to New Jersey Devils 'keeper Martin Brodeur. It was named in 2000.

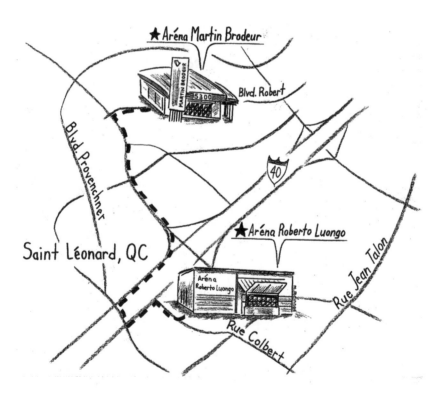

Mr. and Mrs. Umpire

Sade and Wilda Widmeyer were a husband and wife who both became softball umpires. Each made historic contributions to umpiring in Canada.

Sade, sometimes called Guido, created the qualifying exam that all softball umpires in Ontario must now pass. Wilda, who played on the Ontario women's championship teams the Guelph Green Ghosts and the Clifford Swing Skirts, became "North America's first woman umpire." The Widmeyers were inducted together into the Canadian Amateur Softball Hall of Fame in Ottawa in 1997. **The Sade and Wilda Widmeyer Baseball Diamond** is located in Fergus, Ontario.

Sports Pages

The **Andy Zwack Baseball Diamond** in Saskatoon, Saskatchewan, commemorates one of Canada's most important baseball umpires. He wrote three books on the subject: *Basic Baseball Skills: Advanced Training Manual for Managers and Coaches*; *Minor Baseball Umpire's Manual*; and *Guide to Game Procedure in the Interests of Game Conduct and General Discipline*.

His surname may come last in most alphabetical lists, but Zwack served as the first umpire supervisor for the Canadian Federation of Amateur Baseball in the 1960s. One of his students was Wilda Widmeyer, known as "North America's first woman umpire." Zwack was installed in the Saskatchewan Sports Hall of Fame in 1993.

For the Love of the Sport

Eric Coy – who competed mainly in the 1930s and 1940s – was the quintessential amateur athlete. In shot put, javelin, discus, and running, he was so good and set so many records that by the end of his life he was a member of three halls of fame, the Canadian Track and Field Hall of Fame, the Canadian Sports Hall of Fame, and the Manitoba Sports Hall of Fame. His legend remains strong in Winnipeg where the **Eric Coy Arena** and an entire district – the **Eric Coy Neighbourhood** – are named for him.

But apparently, Coy played only for the pure thrill of competition and cared little for the big paycheques and glamour of professional sports. That seems to be the only way of explaining the biggest mystery of his career: Why, despite his superior skills and potential, did he walk away from the Montreal Alouettes in 1945? He played exactly one CFL game with the Alouettes – his only lifetime appearance on a pro roster – before deciding to call it quits. He simply returned to his hometown of Winnipeg – maybe he was homesick – and resumed a humdrum job with the Manitoba Telephone Company. After that, Coy only took part in a few more amateur events before retiring for good.

Klassen's Coin

We all know that the Canadian quarter features the image of the queen on one side and a caribou on the other, right? Well, if any of the coins in your pocket were made in 2010, take a closer look. Instead of that caribou, you might find a picture of Cindy Klassen, namesake of the **Cindy Klassen Recreation Complex** and a street called **Cindy Klassen Way** in Winnipeg, Manitoba.

On January 5, 2010, the Royal Canadian Mint announced it was putting 22 million of the quarters into circulation featuring Klassen in a speed-skating pose in front of a backdrop of a Maple Leaf. The coin celebrates Klassen's record-breaking five-medal performance at the 2006 Winter Olympics in Turin.

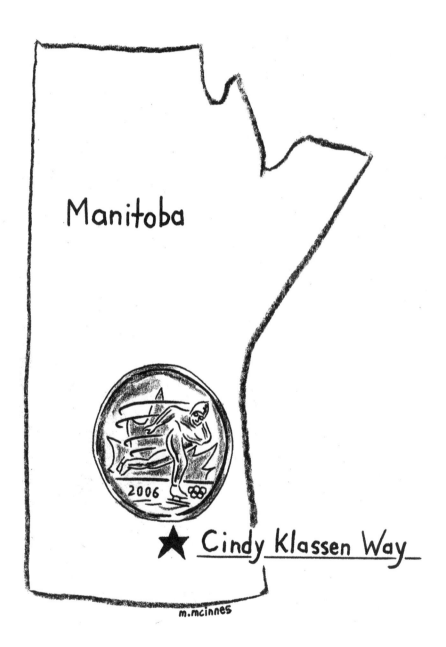

Manitoba

★ Cindy Klassen Way

m.mcinnes

Sports Pages

Elvis Stojko, seven-time Canadian figure skating champion and namesake of the **Elvis Stojko Arena** in Richmond Hill, Ontario, published a book about his career in 1997. It's called *Heart and Soul: Elvis Stojko in his Own Words* and includes more than 200 colour photos.

Hometown Hockey Hero

After his active playing career, Eddie Bush (1918–84) coached the now-defunct Kansas City Scouts of the NHL for one year. His short career as a player lasted two seasons with the Detroit Red Wings.

HOMETOWN TRIBUTE:

Eddie Bush Arena, Collingwood, Ontario.

Get Schooled

If you attend one of these schools, you're in good company. The namesakes of these learning institutes certainly schooled an opponent or two during their athletic careers. In the process, they earned an A+ in the hearts of countless fans. Class is now in session.

- Johnny Bright School, Edmonton, Alberta (football)
- Percy Williams Junior Public School, Toronto, Ontario (track and field)
- Bobby Orr Public School, Oshawa, Ontario (hockey)
- Terry Fox Elementary School, Pierrefonds, Quebec (distance running)
- Terry Fox Junior High School, Calgary, Alberta (distance running)
- Terry Fox Elementary School, Bathurst, New Brunswick (distance running)
- Roger Neilson Public School, Peterborough, Ontario (hockey)
- Herbert H. Carnegie Public School, Maple, Ontario (hockey)

Sites of Local Interest: Part One

Their fame may not be national, or even provincial, but the folks on this page made a lasting mark in the sports communities where they lived and worked. If you're in the neighbourhood, check out these sites of local interest.

The Pat Connolly Press Box: For 25 years, Pat Connolly was the public address announcer at the Halifax Metro Centre, the home rink of the Halifax Citadels of the American Hockey League (AHL) and later the Halifax Mooseheads of the Quebec Major Junior Hockey League (QMJHL). The Metro Centre's press box, where hockey beat writers type up their game reports on laptops, was named after Connolly in September of 2009. **Where to find it:** 1800 Argyle Street, Halifax, Nova Scotia.

McGeachy Fields: New Brunswicker Duncan McGeachy helmed the basketball program at the Canada Winter Games in 1967. According to his New Brunswick Sports Hall of Fame induction citation, "two soccer pitches, a rugby field, three ball diamonds, a 400-metre track, six tennis courts, and a nature walk at St. Stephen's High School are collectively named 'McGeachy Fields' in his honour." **Where to find it:** 282 King Street, St. Stephen, New Brunswick.

The Honourable Ken MacLeod Field: In the courtroom, they called him "Your Honour." Former Saskatchewan politician and judge Ken MacLeod was also a key early organizer of the Regina Little League Association of baseball. For his contributions he was enshrined in the Regina Sports Hall of Fame in 2005. The main baseball diamond at Kiwanis Park now bears his name, including its dignified prefix. **Where to find it:** Corner of Regina Avenue and Montague Street, Regina, Saskatchewan.

The Norm and Jessie Dysart Radiation Centre: This married couple taught and coached at Peterborough's Crestwood Secondary School from 1963 until 1991. In the 1980s, Norm was an assistant coach for Canada's national volleyball team. Today, Crestwood students vie for their school's top sports honour, the Dysart Award. The radiation centre named after Mr. and Mrs. Dysart opened at the Peterborough Regional Health Centre in 2012. **Where to find it:** 1 Hospital Drive, Peterborough, Ontario.

Johnny Copp

A memorial to an unsolved murder that shocked a city isn't the kind of thing you'd expect to find in a church. But the **Johnny Copp Room** at Toronto's Rosedale United Church is just such a place. Johnny Copp was a popular University of Toronto football star who was fatally shot on November 30, 1933. His murderer has never been found.

That Thursday night, Johnny and a friend were studying on the third floor of the Copp residence. Down on the main floor, Johnny's mother was hosting a lively bridge party. As Johnny left the room to make a phone call, he looked out the window and noticed a figure in the shadows. The unknown man seemed to be eyeing the pockets of the guests' clothes thrown across the beds on the second floor. Johnny rushed down the stairs, went out the back door, and confronted the person now purposely hidden in the shadows.

Did You Know?

The Johnny Copp Trophy is awarded each year to the MVP of the University of Toronto Varsity Blues football team. Like the **Johnny Copp Room** at Rosedale United Church, the trophy is named in memory of the former Blues star whose unsolved murder shocked Toronto in 1933.

Notable past winners of the trophy include Bob Coulter, who played quarterback for the Toronto Argonauts in 1936, 1940, and 1941; Ruliff Grass, a member of the Toronto Argonauts Grey Cup–winning team of 1947; and Bill Watters, a former executive with the Toronto Maple Leafs who is now a well-known hockey commentator on Canadian radio and television.

The athletic Johnny Copp could hold his own with almost anyone, but he couldn't have known the burglar was armed. After a struggle, a shot rang out. The burglar fled over the back fence and a wounded Johnny staggered up the porch steps into the house, collapsing on the kitchen floor.

At the hospital, medical experts worked to stop the bleeding. For a while it seemed the 22-year-old would make it, but after numerous transfusions using blood donated by Johnny's football teammates and fraternity friends, he died on Sunday, December 3, the very day he was to address his Sunday school class at

Did You Know?

Three champion Canadian figure skaters have arenas named after them:

- **Elvis Stojko Arena**, Richmond Hill, Ontario: Stojko was the men's Canadian figure skating champion seven times between 1994 and 2002.
- **Elizabeth Manley Arena**, Ottawa, Ontario: Manley captured first place at the women's Canadian figure skating championships in 1985, 1987, and 1988. There is also an **Elizabeth Manley Park** in Ottawa.
- **Kurt Browning Arena**, Caroline, Alberta: Browning, who is from Caroline, was the Canadian men's figure skating champion in 1989, 1990, 1991, and 1993.

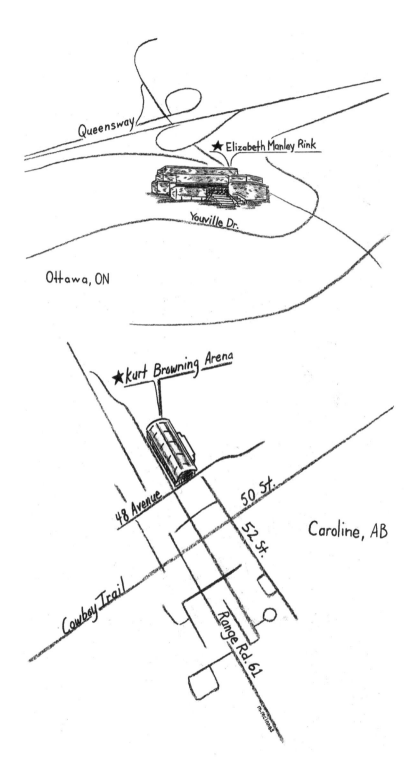

Queensway

★ Elizabeth Manley Rink

Youville Dr.

Ottawa, ON

★ kurt Browning Arena

48 Avenue

50 St.

52 St.

Caroline, AB

Cowboy Trail

Range Rd. 61

In the Name of the Law

John Sopinka, the son of a Hamilton steelworker, was so broke in 1953 he could barely pay his tuition at the University of Toronto. He decided to try out for the Toronto Argonauts as a way of making some money, and to his surprise he made the team! In his two-year CFL career, Sopinka played 29 games with the Toronto Argonauts and eight games with the Montreal Alouettes. He quit after the 1957 season to attend law school.

Sure, it's unlikely that city of Hamilton officials were thinking of Sopinka's football stats when they renovated the derelict former post office on Main Street East and renamed it the **John Sopinka Couthouse** in 1999. After all, Sopinka made his name in the legal profession. He was an outstanding trial lawyer for 28 years and was appointed to the Supreme Court in 1988. The appointment surprised many people, because he was the first person ever chosen to be "a Supreme" who did not have any previous experience as a judge.

Trainer Honoured

Named in April 2007, **Joe Veroni Park** in Guelph is likely the only Canadian place name dedicated to a team trainer. Veroni spent decades on the training staffs of junior and semi-pro hockey teams in Guelph. Perhaps the most famous of those squads was the 1952 Memorial Cup champion Guelph Biltmore Mad Hatters. Featuring future Hall of Famers Andy Bathgate and Harry Howell, the roster that year also included future NHLer Ron Stewart. Veroni was still trainer in 1972 when the team, now called the Guelph CMCs, won the Centennial Cup, the important Junior A title. Future NHLers on the team that year included Doug Risebrough and John Van Boxmeer.

Not Exactly a Tribute of Olympic Proportions?

In 2010, St. Thomas city council announced that Jim Waite, Canada's national and Olympic curling coach, would be recognized for his many achievements, including four trips to the Olympics where his Canadians won two gold medals and two silver medals. Council proclaimed that a parkette at the east end of Lake Margaret would be named in his honour.

But some citizens of the Ontario city were unimpressed with the results. In the *St. Thomas Times-Journal*, one city alderman candidate called the newly created **Jim Waite Park** "an unkempt strip of dandelion-infested land." He noted the park's sign was barely noticeable and added, "the only thing that outnumbers the dandelions on this strip of land is the amount of goose droppings that are strewn throughout. In a word, it is an insult and is certainly no way to recognize anyone, let alone someone of Jim's stature."

To their credit, St. Thomas city officials have since ordered up to $100,000 to be spent on improvements to the park and surrounding area.

Hometown Hockey Hero

A solid defenceman, Alain Côté (1957–) played his entire career, 1977 to 1989, with the Quebec Nordiques. In 696 games, Côté tallied 103 goals and 190 assists.

HOMETOWN TRIBUTE:

Centre sportif Alain-Côté, Matane, Quebec.

Justin Morneau Field

Justin Morneau Field, named after star Minnesota Twins first baseman Justin Morneau, is located at Moody Park in New Westminster, British Columbia. The baseball diamond is a frequent venue for New Westminster Little League games. Morneau, who is from New Westminster, attended the field's official dedication ceremony February 2, 2008. Even though it was in the middle of winter, the former American League MVP still threw out a ceremonial first pitch as family, friends, and members of the public looked on.

Morneau told the *Burnaby News Leader* newspaper that, as a kid, he spent countless happy hours at the Moody Park diamond. As soon as school was over, he would go out and play on the field now named in his honour. It seems that on hot days, swimmers at the outdoor pool next to the field had to stay alert if Justin was taking batting practice. Sometimes, he would accidentally hook a foul ball into the pool.

Thinking back to those days, Morneau did admit that "it was kind of bad because there were actually people in the pool."

Larry Walker Field

New Westminster isn't the only British Columbia city where you can run the bases on a field named for a professional baseball player.

Larry Walker, the greatest Canadian hitter in major league history, is the namesake of **Larry Walker Field** in Maple Ridge, British Columbia. The natural grass ball diamond, one of two fields inside Hammond Park, was named in December of 1992 when Walker was a 26-year-old outfielder in just his third season with the Montreal Expos.

"It's a tremendous honour," said Walker on the day of the naming ceremony. Maple Ridge's faith in the rising star was well placed. Walker would go on to hit 383 home runs and 1,311 RBIs in his amazing 16-year career.

The Hockey-Playing Journalist

Jacques Beauchamp was a *Journal de Montreal* sportswriter who covered the Montreal Canadiens for 30 years. He was so respected for his articles that he was known in the business as the "Dean of Montreal Sportswriters." When Beauchamp was 52, he published a surprising autobiography. It revealed he had done much more than just write about the Habs – the team had actually signed him to a playing contract. The hockey-playing journalist never saw game action but was apparently often pressed into service as goalie during many Canadiens practices. Talk about a reporter getting up close with his interview subjects!

Beauchamp, who died in 1988, still has a place at the Canadiens' home arena. **The Jacques Beauchamp Media Room** is located on the seventh floor of the Bell Centre. The Quebec town of Domaine Vert-Nord has also named the **Parc Jacques Beauchamp** after him.

Mr. Badminton

Badminton champion Jack Purcell – namesake of Ottawa's **Jack Purcell Lane** – was inducted into the Canadian Olympic Hall of Fame in 1973 despite never playing a single match at the Olympic Games. In fact, badminton was not even an Olympic sport at the time of his induction. How did that happen? In selecting Purcell, the Canadian Olympic

Committee explained that, based on his brilliant role as a builder of the sport in Canada and the world, he should be inducted anyway.

Horsing Around

Human athletes aren't the only ones with Canadian places named after them. In Toronto, the names of two thoroughbred race horses can be found on street signs. **Northern Dancer Boulevard** is a tribute to the 1968 winner of the Kentucky Derby, while **Nearctic Drive** is a nod to Nearctic, the 1956 winner of the Victoria Stakes and the Michigan Mile.

Historic Arena

William Allman Arena in Stratford, Ontario, is just one of the many sports facilities across Canada named after people only known locally. These individuals are often not athletes themselves, but have dedicated their lives to local sports. This arena, one of the oldest operating arenas in the world, was named in 1996 for Bill Allman, the rink manager there for an astonishing 47 years. A list has been made of the NHL players that played junior hockey there. It includes George Hay, Nick Libbet, Craig Hartsburg, Ed Olczyk, Nelson Emerson, Rob Blake, Chris Pronger, Tim Taylor, Dave Shaw, Mike Peluso, Louis DeBrusk, Brian Smolinski, Marc Potvin, Kevin Dahl, Greg De Vries, Garth Snow, Rem Murray, Mike Watt, and Boyd Devereaux.

Steve Omischl

The **Steve Omischl Sports Field Complex**, which officially opened in North Bay on August 20, 2011, is named after one of the most accomplished skiers in Canadian history. Born and raised in North Bay, aerials specialist Steve Omischl won 40 medals in World Cup ski competitions during his career.

The Steve Omischl Sports Field Complex doesn't include any ski lifts, moguls, or alpine hills, but it does feature three top-quality soccer fields and three tournament-calibre baseball diamonds. The impressive sports facility cost $11.7 million to build. To get there, follow North Bay's Lakeshore Drive and hang a right just past Booth Road. You can't **misch** it.

"This is all my athletic accomplishments put together," Omischl told the *North Bay Nugget* newspaper about the opening of the facility. "It's very flattering to know that people followed my career and cared that much that they wanted to honour me in this way."

The Dean of Canadian Sportscasters

Henry Viney, nicknamed the "Dean of Canadian Sportscasters," was inducted into the Alberta Sports Hall of Fame in 1983. Often seen with his trademark cigar, Viney spent most of his radio career with the Calgary stations CJOC and CFCN. His hall of fame biography states that Viney "described the fistic exploits of boxers such as Rocky Marciano, Jersey Joe Walcott, and Floyd Patterson" as well as "Kentucky Derbies, Indy 500s, Olympic Games, Pan Am Games, Grey Cups, Stanley Cups, and World Series." According to stories, Viney personally saw more than 10,000 games of amateur baseball and junior and midget hockey. **Henry Viney Arena** is located in Calgary, Alberta.

Hometown Hockey Hero

Born in Montreal, Rod Gilbert (1941–) would play nearly two decades as a member of the New York Rangers, scoring 406 career regular season goals. In 1979, his number 7 became the first number ever retired by the Rangers. Gilbert acquired membership in the Hockey Hall of Fame in 1982.

HOMETOWN TRIBUTE:

Aréna Rodrigue-Gilbert, Montreal, Quebec.

Dynamiter

After graduating from university in Montreal, Max Bell signed a contract with the Kimberley Dynamiters, a little-known semi-pro team in 1930s British Columbia. League records from the time are so scarce that Bell's point totals and even what position he played are unclear.

But Bell didn't stay in Kimberley for long. With a knack for business, he would go on to gain notoriety as the owner of a newspaper empire that spanned Canada. But ink never completely replaced Bell's interest in ice. He was one of the first people ever to invest in the Vancouver Canucks. Also a horse racing enthusiast, Bell was the owner of Meadow Court, the horse that won the Irish Derby in 1965. **The Max Bell Aquatic Centre** at the University of Lethbridge, opened in 1986, is named after him. There is also a **Max Bell Arena** in Calgary.

Deaf Athlete Recognized

Former Ottawa mail carrier Paul Landry is the winningest deaf athlete in Canadian history. After joining the Ottawa Deaf Sports Club, Landry became an inspiration for other hearing-impaired athletes in the 1980s. At the deaf equivalent of the Olympic Games, he won a silver medal in 1981 in West Germany, a gold medal in 1984 in Los Angeles, and a bronze in 1989 in New Zealand, all in track and field events. In 1993, the city of Ottawa recognized his achievements by renaming Uplands South Park in his honour. It's now called **Paul Landry Park**.

1972, Paul Henderson Street, Erin Mills, Ontario

Paul Henderson famously scored the winning goal for Canada in the thrilling 1972 Summit Series victory against the Russians. Now kids near Mississauga, Ontario, can score their own winning goals – street hockey style – on the street named after him. **Paul Henderson Street** in Erin Mills, Ontario, was officially named in early 2005.

That's not the only southern Ontario place name tribute to Henderson. On September 30, 2011, a hockey rink at Tomken Twin Arena in Mississauga was renamed in honour of the Team Canada hero. The sign affixed above the door leading to the ice surface now reads in blue lettering "Paul Henderson Rink." That has a nicer ring to it than the previous name – "Rink One."

Foreign Affairs

In the United States city of Draper, Utah, "**Mike Weir Drive**" isn't a reference to Canadian golfer Mike Weir's shot from a fairway onto a green. It's the name of a street. Weir, who grew up in Brights Grove, Ontario, now lives with his wife and two daughters in Draper.

Hometown Hockey Hero

In his brilliant rookie year, his only NHL season, Michel Briére (1949–71) recorded 44 points in 76 games. That summer, the Pittsburgh Penguins star was involved in a car crash near Malartic, Quebec. He died 11 months later from his injuries. The Penguins officially retired Briére's number 21 in 2001.

HOMETOWN TRIBUTE:

Centre Michel Briére, Malartic, Quebec.

Oxford University Ice Hockey Club

When people think of English sports, it's soccer, not hockey, that probably comes to mind. But England's most famous university, Oxford, has actually had its own hockey team since 1885. In the 1920s, three outstanding Canadians who now have buildings named after them were members of the Oxford Blues at the same time. Future prime minister Lester B. Pearson, future governor general Roland Michener, and R.H.G. Bonnycastle, later a fur trader and publisher, were each attending Oxford on scholarships when they were teammates in 1923. With so much Canadian content, is it any wonder the team won the Spengler Cup in Switzerland that year?

Places named after Lester B. Pearson (1897–1972)

- Lester Pearson Memorial High School, Wesleyville, Newfoundland and Labrador
- Lester B. Pearson College of the Pacific, Pedder Bay, British Columbia
- Mount Lester Pearson, Caribou Land District, British Columbia
- Lester B. Pearson High School, Calgary, Alberta
- Lester B. Pearson Street, Woodbridge, Ontario
- Lester B. Pearson Street, Kleinberg, Ontario
- Lester B. Pearson International Airport, Toronto, Ontario
- Lester B. Pearson High School, Burlington, Ontario
- Lester B. Pearson Park, St. Catharines, Ontario
- Lester B. Pearson Public School, Ajax, Ontario
- Lester B. Pearson Park, Ajax, Ontario
- Lester B. Pearson School, Brampton, Ontario
- Lester B. Pearson Catholic Secondary School, Gloucester, Ontario
- Lester B. Pearson School for the Arts, London, Ontario
- Lester B. Pearson School, Waterloo, Ontario
- Lester B. Pearson School, Aurora, Ontario
- Lester B. Pearson Elementary School, Toronto, Ontario
- Lester B. Pearson School, Saskatoon, Saskatchewan

Places named for Roland Michener (1900–91)

- Roland Michener Arena, Winnipeg, Manitoba
- Roland Michener School, Saskatoon, Saskatchewan
- Michener Crescent, Saskatoon, Saskatchewan
- Roland Michener Elementary School, Calgary, Alberta
- Roland Michener Junior High School, Slave Lake, Alberta
- Roland Michener Centre, Red Deer, Alberta
- Roland Michener Park/Public School, Ajax, Ontario
- Roland Michener School, South Porcupine, Ontario

- Roland Michener School, Kanata, Ontario
- Mount Michener, Alberta

Places named for R.H.G. Bonnycastle (1903–68)

- R.H.G. Bonnycastle School, Winnipeg, Manitoba
- Bonnycastle Park, Winnipeg, Manitoba

Is That Even a Sport?

On June 3, 1983, the University of Toronto recognized its most famous professor, the literary critic Northrop Frye, by naming one of its buildings **Northrop Frye Hall**. Frye was called "the foremost living student of Western literature" for the many books he wrote about history's great authors.

Less well known is that Frye got his start not as a writer but as a competitive typist. He was a typing whiz at his New Brunswick high school in the pre-computer days of the 1920s. At 16, he travelled to Toronto for the first time to compete in the Canadian National Typing Contest organized by the Underwood Typewriter Company. In his event, held at Massey Hall on April 8, 1929, Frye won second place in the novice division of the contest. He typed 63 words a minute.

Wait a second. Is competitive typing even a sport? You decide.

Burgers, Baseball ... Bailey

In the 1930s, an American named Nat Bailey started opening hamburger restaurants around Vancouver. One of them was the first drive-through restaurant in Canada. It turns out that Nat, who had cheered for the Twins as a kid back in Minnesota, was a big baseball fan. But Canada had no big league teams and it would be years before the arrival of the Toronto Blue Jays and the Montreal Expos.

So Nat did the next best thing. With his business going well, he simply bought a Triple-A team from the United States and installed it in Vancouver, giving it the very Canadian name, the Vancouver Mounties. The Mounties became a farm team for the Baltimore Orioles, the Milwaukee Braves, and his beloved Minnesota Twins. Shortly after Bailey died in 1978, Vancouver's Capilano Stadium was renamed **Nat Bailey**

Stadium as a nod to his contribution to baseball in Canada. Fruits and vegetables are also sold weekly at the **Nat Bailey Farmer's Market**.

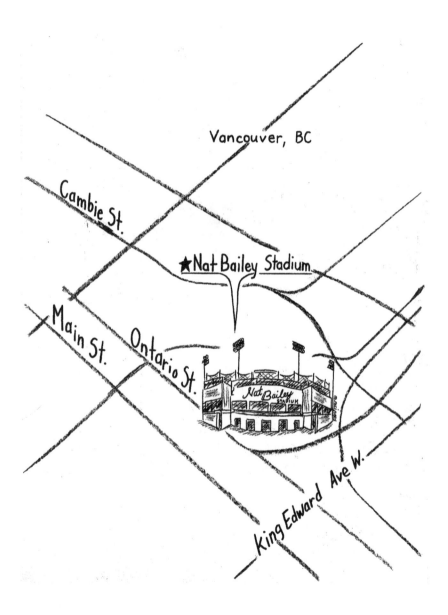

Hometown Hockey Hero

After getting an aeronautical engineering degree from New York's Rensselaer Polytechnic Institute, Joé Juneau (1968–) began an NHL hockey career that included stints with the Boston Bruins, Ottawa Senators, and four other teams. In 13 seasons, he scored 156 goals.

HOMETOWN TRIBUTE:

Aréna Joé-Juneau, Pont-Rouge, Quebec.

Hometown Hockey Heroes: Part One

Like the other Hometown Hockey Heroes in this book, the players discussed below have places named after them back home. Many are in Quebec and Ontario. Those who lace up their skates in these arenas can draw extra inspiration from the illustrious hockey names emblazoned on the sign out front.

A defenceman, **Leo Boivin** (1932–) played 19 seasons in the NHL, mostly with the Toronto Maple Leafs, and was inducted into the Hockey Hall of Fame in 1986. **Hometown tribute:** Leo Boivin Community Centre, Prescott, Ontario.

Marcel Bonin (1931–) scored 97 goals, notched 175 assists, and won four Stanley Cups in his NHL career. He played for the Detroit Red Wings, Boston Bruins, and Montreal Canadiens. **Hometown tribute:** Centre récréatif Marcel-Bonin, Joliette, Quebec.

Hall of Famer **Ray Bourque** (1960–) played 21 seasons with the Boston Bruins. Still seeking his first Stanley Cup after 21 seasons in Beantown, Bourque moved to the Colorado Avalanche in 1999 and finally won the Cup in 2001. **Hometown tribute:** Aréna Raymond-Bourque, Saint-Laurent, Quebec.

Hockey writer Stan Fischler called **John Tonelli** (1957–) a "veritable whirling dervish on skates." With the New York Islanders dynasty of the 1980s, Tonelli's tough style of play helped the team win four Stanley Cups in a row. He hit triple digits in points in 1984–85, the same year his hometown renamed the generic-sounding Community Sports Complex in his honour. **Hometown tribute:** John Tonelli Arena, Milton, Ontario.

Yvan Cournoyer (1943–) played for the Montreal Canadiens from 1963 to 1979, winning the Stanley Cup ten times. Cournoyer and fellow NHL great Marcel Dionne both have hockey arenas named after them in their hometown of Drummondville. **Hometown tribute:** Olympia Yvan-Cournoyer, Drummondville, Quebec.

Goalie **Terry Sawchuk** (1929–1970) racked up 103 career shutouts for the Detroit Red Wings and four other teams – a record that stood till 2009. The Winnipegger's 172 career ties may never be equalled in an era where shootouts now routinely decide winners. The events surrounding Sawchuk's death at age 40 while a member of the New York Rangers are explored in a number of books, including *Sawchuk: The Troubles and Triumphs of the World's Greatest Goalie* by David Dupuis. **Hometown tribute:** Terry Sawchuk Arena, Winnipeg, Manitoba.

Right winger **Murray Balfour** (1936–65) recorded 157 points in 306 career games, mostly with the Chicago Black Hawks. His career was tragically cut short by his early death at age 28. **Hometown tribute:** Murray Balfour Arena, Regina, Saskatchewan.

Despite playing only seven seasons in the NHL, all with the Montreal Canadiens, **Bill Durnan** (1916–72) is one of the legendary goalies of yesteryear. He retired at age 35 and was inducted into the Hockey Hall of Fame in 1964. **Hometown tribute:** Aréna Bill Durnan, Montreal, Quebec.

One of the great defenceman in NHL history, **Doug Harvey** (1924–89) struggled with personal troubles during and after his illustrious playing career that spanned from 1945 until 1969. But by the late 1980s, he was welcomed back to the Canadiens organization as a scout. His number 2 sweater was retired by the Montreal Canadiens to honour his 13 years with the club. **Hometown tribute:** Aréna Doug Harvey, Montreal, Quebec.

A dependable point-getter during his NHL career, **Réjean Houle** (1949–) played 11 seasons with the Montreal Canadiens, garnering five Stanley Cup rings with the team. Later, as Habs GM, he orchestrated the trade that sent goalie Patrick Roy to Colorado for Jocelyn Thibault, Martin Rucinsky, and Andrei Kovalenko. **Hometown tribute:** Aréna Réjean Houle, Rouyn-Noranda, Quebec.

The Mystery of the Jenkins Cup

Every Canadian sports fan is familiar with the NHL's Stanley Cup and the CFL's Grey Cup. But have you heard of the Jenkins Cup? It existed for such a short time that few people know anything about it.

Like **Fergie Jenkins Parkway** and **Fergie Jenkins Park** in Chatham, Ontario, the Jenkins Cup was named in honour of Canadian-born Hall of Fame pitcher Ferguson Jenkins. It was created in 2003 to be awarded each year to the champion of the Canadian Baseball League.

Unfortunately, the Canadian Baseball League went broke halfway through its first season and had to suspend operations.

All remaining games were cancelled. A team called the Calgary Outlaws was declared league champs based on their record, but the Jenkins Cup was never actually awarded amid the confusion of the CBL's demise. Instead, it apparently vanished when the league collapsed and has been missing ever since. Efforts to find it have come up empty.

Perhaps someday a sports-minded sleuth will track down this historic piece of baseball silverware.

The Monday Night Miracle

Doug Wickenheiser – namesake of the **Doug Wickenheiser Arena** in Regina, Saskatchewan – scored 115 goals in his NHL career. None are more famous than the one he scored in overtime on May 12, 1986, in a game known as the Monday Night Miracle.

That night, while trailing 5–2 in the third period, Wickenheiser and the St. Louis Blues pulled off an unlikely comeback victory in a big playoff game against the Calgary Flames.

Seven minutes into overtime, Wickenheiser collected a rebound in front of the Calgary net and fired a shot past goalie Mike Vernon for the winning goal, stunning the Flames and delighting the delirious home crowd in St. Louis with a 6–5 victory.

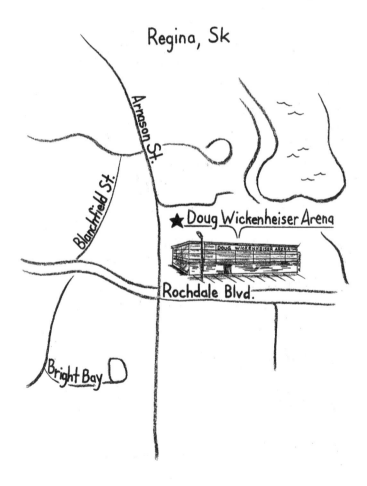

Did You Know?

Elite hockey runs in the Wickenheiser family. Doug Wickenheiser's younger cousin, Hayley Wickenheiser, is one of Canada's most recognizable athletes and has been called the best female ice hockey player in the world. Hayley, who was 20 years old when her NHLer cousin died of cancer in 1999, helped lead Canada to thrilling medal wins at the 1998, 2002, 2006, and 2010 Olympics. Like Doug, Hayley is also part of Canada's sports geography. In July of 2006, her hometown of Shaunavon, Saskatchewan, renamed its sportsplex **Wickenheiser Place** in her honour. The following year, the Calgary community of Silver Springs dedicated an outdoor rink in her name, calling it **Hayley's Rink**.

Got 21 Seconds? Witness the Quickness

Bill Mosienko, the player who scored the fastest hat trick in NHL history, was a true Winnipegger whose fellow citizens dubbed him "the Pride of the North End." Since the former Keewatin Arena was renamed for Mosienko in 1991, a special bronze plaque describing the former Chicago Blackhawk's career has adorned a wall of the facility. Can you read it in less time than it took Mosienko to accomplish his triple-fast-action goal-scoring speed record?

Billy Mosienko Arena
Dedication December 30, 1991

THE PRIDE OF THE NORTH END
William (Billy) Mosienko is acknowledged as being one

of the top hockey players of his era as well as being one of Manitoba's finest contributions to the National Hockey League. Born in Winnipeg on November 2, 1921, he grew up in the North End where he played the majority of his minor hockey.

Bill played 711 games in the NHL, scoring 258 goals with 282 assists. As well as appearing in 5 All-Star games, he also won the Lady Byng Trophy (Sportsmanship) in 1945. **The record books reveal one of his greatest accomplishments occurred when he scored 3 goals within 21 seconds in New York against the Rangers on March 23, 1952.**

Bill has been inducted into the Hockey Hall of Fame in 1965 and the Manitoba Sports Hall of Fame in 1980. At the completion of his professional hockey career Bill remained a resident of North Winnipeg, as well as retaining a business interest in the community through the ownership of a bowling alley.

Hometown Hockey Hero

Ted "Teeder" Kennedy (1925–2009) spent his entire career with the Toronto Maple Leafs. He was the first player to win the Stanley Cup five times and the first rookie to score a Stanley Cup–winning goal. His faceoff skills are still legendary among hockey experts.

HOMETOWN TRIBUTE:

Teeder Kennedy Youth Arena, Port Colborne, Ontario.

Miracle on Manchester

Mario Lessard – namesake of the **Aréna Mario Lessard** in East Broughton, Quebec – was the goalie for the Los Angeles Kings on April 10, 1982, when the Kings pulled off one the biggest NHL playoff comebacks of all time; ever since, the game has been known as the Miracle on Manchester. At that time, the Kings home arena was located on Manchester Boulevard, just outside Los Angeles.

The underdog Kings were losing badly that night in their playoff game against Wayne Gretzky and the powerhouse Edmonton Oilers. Kings fans were quiet as they watched the Oilers put five pucks behind Lessard to gain a 5–0 lead by the third period. But overconfident, the Oilers couldn't hold on. The suddenly energetic Kings scored five goals, and Lessard stopped a breakaway in the dying minutes to force overtime.

As overtime began, a daring early play by Lessard almost backfired. After skating far from his crease for a puck, he slid to the ice in a collision with the Oilers' Glenn Anderson and found himself helplessly out of position. With the net wide open, the Oilers had a golden opportunity to win the game. Somehow, a backhander from the Oilers' Mark Messier sailed high. Lessard and the Kings were still alive. When they scored two minutes later to win, it capped a historic comeback, and Kings fans erupted in pandemonium.

Hometown Hockey Hero

A teenager when he entered the NHL, Hamilton-born Dave Andreychuk was well past his 40th birthday when, as a member of the Tampa Bay Lightning, he played his first game in a Stanley Cup final. He's still the oldest player to make such a championship debut. The former Toronto Maple Leaf and Buffalo Sabre is the league's all-time leader in total power-play goals scored (274).

HOMETOWN TRIBUTE:

Dave Andreychuk Mountain Arena, Hamilton, Ontario
(officially named July 30, 2004).

American Invasion

Milt Stegall of the Winnipeg Blue Bombers broke the CFL touchdown record in 2007. To the delight of fans, Winnipeg City Council soon announced plans to rename a local street in his honour. It didn't matter that Stegall is an American, born in Cincinnati, Ohio, in 1970. At the official dedication ceremony on September 5, 2008, the U.S. citizen told a crowd of media, politicians, and the public, "It's an honour and a privilege that I'll be a part of Winnipeg forever!"

Stegall is not the only American-born CFL player with a Canadian place name to his credit. Emery Barnes, born in Louisiana in 1929, played three years for the BC Lions, including 1965, when the team won the Grey Cup. **Emery Barnes Park** in Vancouver was officially unveiled September 27, 2003.

Johnny Bright, born in Fort Wayne, Indiana, in 1930, joined the Edmonton Eskimos in the 1950s. He became the CFL's all-time rushing leader and won three Grey Cups. **Johnny Bright School** officially opened September 15, 2010. **Johnny Bright**

Stadium, home of the Edmonton Raiders minor football team, is also in Edmonton.

Bernie Faloney, born in Carnegie, Pennsylvania, in 1932, is one of the great quarterbacks in Hamilton Tiger-Cats history and a member of the Canadian Football Hall of Fame. Part of Hamilton's Cannon Street near Ivor Wynne Stadium is known as **Bernie Faloney Way**.

Are You Gonna Go My Way?

During their careers, the athletes and coaches on this list showed us the **way** it's done. Even though some are now a**way** from the limelight, they're still leading the **way**. To that we say, **way** to go! (By the **way**, thanks for finding your **way** to this page.)

- Cindy Klassen Way, Winnipeg, Manitoba (speed skating)
- Mike Richards Way, Kenora, Ontario (hockey)
- Terry Fox Way, Mississauga, Ontario, and Vancouver, British Columbia (distance running)
- Wayne Gretzky Way, Edmonton, Alberta (hockey)
- Kate Pace Way, North Bay, Ontario (skiing)
- Pat Quinn Way, Hamilton, Ontario (hockey)
- Sandra Schmirler Way, Regina, Saskatchewan (curling)
- James Naismith Way, Almonte, Ontario (basketball)
- Roger Neilson Way, Peterborough, Ontario (hockey)

Media Gondolas

A few NHL arenas have named broadcast booths after highly respected play-by-play announcers. These booths, or gondolas, are where the announcers and colour commentators sit while they call the games from high above the ice.

- The **Foster Hewitt Media Gondola** is located at the Air Canada Centre, the home arena of the Toronto Maple Leafs. Hewitt, who died in 1985, is probably the most famous sports broadcaster in Canadian history.
- The **Jim Robson Broadcast Gondola** is located at Rogers Arena, the home of the Vancouver Canucks. Robson was the television voice of the Canucks from the 1970s to the 1990s.
- The **Ed Whalen Broadcast Gondola** is situated at the Scotiabank Saddledome (formerly known as the Pengrowth Saddledome), the home of the Calgary Flames. Whalen called the first Calgary Flames game in 1980 and remained the television voice of the team until 1999. Whalen, who died in 1999, was equally known during his career as the long-time host of Stampede Wrestling television broadcasts. The **Ed Whalen Ice Rink** at Southland Leisure Centre in Calgary, Alberta, is also named for him.

Hometown Hockey Hero

André Lacroix (1945–) was a point-scoring machine for several World Hockey Association teams in the 1970s. He played well during his NHL years, as well, leading the Philadelphia Flyers in scoring at the end of the 1960s and at the beginning of the 1970s.

HOMETOWN TRIBUTE:

Aréna André Lacroix, Lévis, Quebec.

McLuhan's Oar

Marshall McLuhan Way, a small street near the University of Toronto (U of T), is named for the famous Canadian media theorist who coined the terms "global village" and "the medium is the message."

Professor McLuhan's office at U of T in the 1960s was a weird and wonderful place. It was filled with his favourite things, including a death mask of the poet John Keats, a giant abstract mural that captured the effects of television on the modern world, and – as many puzzled visitors noted over the years – a large oar prominently displayed over McLuhan's desk.

Few were aware the professor had rowed on Cambridge University teams as a young Canadian scholarship student in England in the 1930s. According to a biographer, McLuhan never made the fastest two or three boats in his college, but in the spring term of 1936, he did row in the fifth-fastest boat. His squad did well enough in the races that each member was entitled to keep his oar in keeping with Cambridge tradition. This Cambridge oar remained one of McLuhan's most cherished souvenirs his entire life.

Sweet 16

Larry Hillman is the youngest player *to have his named engraved* on the Stanley Cup. He was only 18 years, two months, and nine days old when his Detroit Red Wings won the Cup in 1955. But is Hillman the youngest-ever *winner* of the Stanley Cup?

Percival Molson is almost certainly the youngest person to win the trophy. He was only 16 years and 135 days old when he won the Cup with the Montreal Victorias in 1896. In those days, players' names were not inscribed on the Cup. Today, the Montreal Alouettes of the CFL play their home games at **Percival Molson Stadium**, which officially opened in 1919.

Coach Kilrea

On October 14, 1967, Brian Kilrea scored the first goal in Los Angeles Kings franchise history in a game against the Philadelphia Flyers. After that night, Kilrea would only play 24 more games in the NHL.

Instead, Kilrea found a job teaching the game to others, beginning a career that would make him the winningest coach in minor league history. His 1,193 victories behind the bench of the OHL Ottawa 67s stands as an all-time record. In Ottawa, both the **Brian Kilrea Room** at the Children's Hospital and **Brian Kilrea Arena** are named after him.

Hometown Hockey Hero

The little Quebec town of Thurso, closer to Ottawa than Montreal, is where you'll find the arena named for Canadiens great Guy Lafleur (1951–). Lafleur scored more than 500 goals and surpassed the 1,000-point plateau in his career. He won five Stanley Cups and was inducted into the Hockey Hall of Fame in 1988.

HOMETOWN TRIBUTE:

Aréna Guy-Lafleur, Thurso, Quebec.

Skull and Bones

The Skull and Bones fraternity based at Yale University in New Haven, Connecticut, is one of the most talked about secret societies in the world. It was founded in 1832 and its members, known as "bonesmen," are sworn to secrecy about their rituals, initiation ceremonies, and the many stolen artifacts they are said to own, including the skulls of former U.S. president Martin Van Buren, American Indian chief Geronimo, and the Mexican general Pancho Villa. Former Skull and Bones members include U.S. presidents and a long list of bigwigs in politics and business.

It's a little-known fact that one Canadian building is named after a bonesman. Ben Avery was a star athlete at Yale in the 1910s. He was captain of the Yale Bulldogs wrestling squad and an offensive end on the football team for two years, being chosen All-American in 1913. When he moved to Canada, he became president of the Canadian Forestry Association. You can read about Avery on a plaque below a bronze statue of him in the lobby of the **Ben F. Avery Gymnasium** at Laurentian University in Sudbury, Ontario.

Sir Casimir Gzowski Park, Toronto

How did a Polish count end up with a popular park on the shores of Lake Ontario named after him? It all started in Eastern Europe way back in 1830 when Polish officers and civilians revolted against Russia. A newly graduated young engineer and nobleman named Casimir Gzowski was among the rebels. According to stories, Gzowski was wounded in a battle, taken prisoner, and then forced to flee to North America.

In Canada, this highly educated son of the Polish count Stanislaw Gzowski of Grodno became a rich and famous engineer. The Welland Canal and the St. Lawrence and Atlantic Railway were among his best handiwork. A personal friend of prime minister Sir John A Macdonald, Gzowski was made lieutenant governor of Ontario in 1896.

Meanwhile, Gzowski had organized the Dominion Rifle Association to give part-time Canadian soldiers a chance to practise their shooting skills. But it was really more of a sporting association, and each year it sent a team to an imperial shooting competition at Wimbledon, England. In the Canadian national competitions, marksmen of the association vied for the Gzowski Cup. Another sports connection for Gzowski: he co-founded the Ontario Jockey Club for horse racing in 1881.

Sports Pages

At 23, Scott Young was told by a grouchy editor in Manitoba, "You'll never be worth more than $25 a week to the *Winnipeg Free Press!*"

Young didn't mope very long about the put-down. Instead, he moved to Ontario and launched one of the most successful sportswriting careers Canada's ever seen. He covered everything from Grey Cups to the Olympics for *Sports Illustrated* and the *Globe and Mail*, guest hosted *Hockey Night in Canada*, and also found time to write 45 books. He was rewarded with a special spot in the Hockey Hall of Fame's media section in 1988 and the naming of **Scott Young Public School** in Omemee, Ontario, followed in 1993.

Not bad for a guy who couldn't get a raise in the 'Peg.

Look for Young's best-known books for kids, the trilogy of page-turner hockey novels that includes *Scrubs on Skates*, *Boy on Defence*, and *A Boy at Leafs Camp*. These books about the struggles of teenage hockey players are classically Canadian.

Sports Sites Factoid:

Scott Young is the father of legendary Canadian musician Neil Young. Keep on rockin' in the free world!

Hometown Hockey Hero

Former Hartford Whaler and Detroit Red Wing Dave Barr (1960–) played 614 regular season NHL games in the 1980s and 1990s. He was later an assistant coach with the Colorado Avalanche.

HOMETOWN TRIBUTE:

Dave Barr Arena, Grand Prairie, Alberta.

Roll Up the Brimb to Win

Earl Brimblecombe, who made his living directing a courier service called Lightning Delivery, was a well-known figure in Guelph, Ontario, for many years. **Earl Brimblecombe Park** on Willow Road in Guelph stands as a lasting tribute to his community involvement. Unveiled in 1998 when the late Brimblecombe was still a spry 72, the park is a memorial to a man who was president of the Guelph Minor Hockey Association and a long-time member of the Guelph Referees Association. R.I.P., Mr. Ref.

Hometown Hockey Hero

Fred Barrett (1950–) suited up for 745 NHL hockey games in his career, which included stays with the Minnesota North Stars and Los Angeles Kings.

HOMETOWN TRIBUTE:

Fred Barrett Arena, Ottawa, Ontario.

Sites of Local Interest: Part Two

Their fame may not be national, or even provincial, but the folks on this page made a lasting mark in the sports communities where they lived and worked. If you're in the neighbourhood, check out these four sites of local interest.

Wynand Groen Gym: Known to many as "Mr. Hoops," Wynand Groen coached elementary school basketball in the St. Catharines, Ontario, area for 32 years. During that span, his purple-and-gold-uniformed players at St. Davids Public School won four Ontario basketball titles. In 1997, the *St. Catharines Standard* newspaper gave him the Jack Gatecliff Award for dedication to sport. The gymnasium at St. Davids was renamed in Groen's honour on October 15, 2010. **Where to find it:** 1344 York Road, St. Davids, Ontario.

Robert Barr Football Field: On November 2, 2011, Ottawa mayor Jim Watson led a small renaming ceremony at the sportsfield near the Kanata Recreation Complex. That day the field officially became known as the Robert Barr

Football Field. Barr was recognized for his many years as coach of the Kanata Knights Football Club for players ages 8–16. A news headline that day read "Football Field Named After Local Legend." **Where to find it:** 100 Walter Baker Place, Kanata, Ontario.

The Ken Bahnuk Lounge: The moniker for Laurentian University sports teams is "The Voyageurs." Players are familiar with the Ken Bahnuk Lounge – centrally located in the main athletic building – but few know much about its namesake. A track and field specialist, Ken Bahnuk was the 1972 recipient of the Special Voyageur Award, presented yearly to "an individual, athlete or non-athlete, who has made an outstanding contribution to the pride and tradition of Laurentian Athletics." **Where to find it:** 10 Athletic Building Road, Laurentian Campus, Sudbury, Ontario.

Ned Andreoni Gymnasium: Originally from the United States, Ned Andreoni moved to Moose Jaw in 1967 to play baseball for the minor league Moose Jaw Regals. He never moved back to sunny California. Instead, he made the chillier climes of Saskatchewan his permanent home, and after his stint with the Regals, coached the Vanier Vikings basketball team at Moose Jaw's Vanier Collegiate for an amazing 35 years. The Vikings' home court is now called the Ned Andreoni Gymnasium. **Where to find it:** 324 MacDonald Street West, Moose Jaw, Saskatchewan.

Schmirler the Curler

When three-time Canadian women's curling champ Sandra Schmirler died of cancer at age 37 in 2000, her funeral was broadcast live on two television networks. It had been just two years since her big gold medal win at the 1998 Olympics in Nagano, Japan.

In tribute to the woman known as "Schmirler the Curler," three Canadian spaces were named after her within months of the funeral ceremony. The first was the **Sandra Schmirler Olympic Gold Park** in her hometown of Biggar, Saskatchewan, on August 6, 2000. **The Sandra Schmirler Leisure Centre** and **Sandra Schmirler Way**, both in Regina, were unveiled soon after.

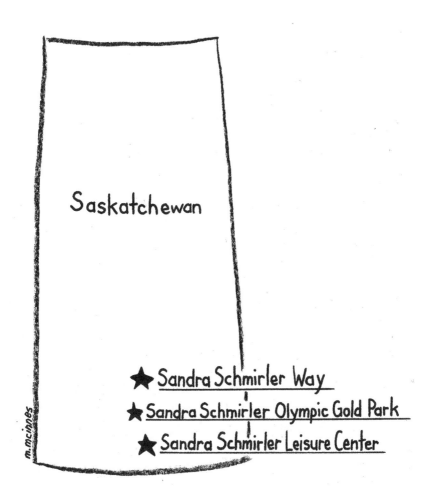

Hometown Hockey Hero

The nearly anagrammatically named defenceman Mario Marois (1957–) enjoyed a long NHL career. His best years were the 1980s seasons he spent with the Quebec Nordiques and Winnipeg Jets, posting career highs in games played and points.

HOMETOWN TRIBUTE:

Amphiglace Mario Marois, Ancienne-Lorette, Quebec.

Limpert's Lane

Stay in your lane and swim as fast as you can. In a nutshell, that about sums up the game plan if you aim to win races in water. It's what Canadian swimmer Marianne Limpert did on July 26, 1996, at the Summer Olympics in Atlanta. In the 200-metre individual medley event that day, super speedy swimmers from Sweden, Ireland, Australia, and five other countries occupied the pool's eight lanes. Wearing the Maple Leaf on her swim cap, Limpert stayed in her lane, swam as fast as she could, and won a much-deserved silver medal for Canada with a time of 2:14:35.

Twelve days later, when Limpert's overjoyed home city of Fredericton, New Brunswick, celebrated by naming a street in her honour, they didn't call it a road, an avenue, or a drive. Appropriately, they called it a lane. **Limpert Lane** was officially unveiled in a ceremony on August 6, 1996, and is now part of the scenic riverfront walkway in Fredericton. Interviewed by the Canadian Broadcasting Corporation, the swift swimmer quipped, "I would appreciate it if Limpert Lane didn't have a speed limit."

Coming Up Rose's

Spectators arriving for sports events at the Hershey Centre, the home rink of the Mississauga St. Michael's Majors of the Ontario Hockey League, may notice something familiar-sounding about the address. The Hershey Centre is located at **5500 Rose Cherry Place**. The street is named after the late wife of Don Cherry, the unmistakable hockey commentator who can be seen every Saturday night with host Ron McLean on *Hockey Night in Canada*'s "Coach's Corner."

Don was the owner and founder of the Mississauga Ice Dogs, the first team to occupy the Hershey Centre when it opened back in 1998. As a tribute, Don convinced city officials to name the road leading into the new building after Rose, who had recently passed away after battling cancer.

Hometown Hockey Hero

Marcel Dionne, who netted 731 goals in his 18-season NHL career, currently sits fourth on the all-time goal-scoring list. Nicknamed "the Little Beaver," Dionne broke in with the Detroit Red Wings but in 1975 was traded to the Los Angeles Kings. Sporting the distinct purple and gold of the classic Kings uniform, Dionne routinely led his team in scoring.

HOMETOWN TRIBUTE:

The Marcel Dionne Centre, Drummondville, Quebec.

Rodeo Raymond

At age 29, Raymond Knight came up with an idea for a new kind of sporting event for ranchers and cowboys. He announced that Raymond, Alberta, a town he shares his name with, would host the event. He even invented a new word for it: a "stampede." The year was 1902 – ten years before the first Calgary Stampede. Knight won the steer roping event at that first competition.

Knight, who died in 1947, was inducted into the Canadian Professional Rodeo Hall of Fame in 1982. Today Raymond's town motto is "Home of the First Stampede," and its multi-sport fields have long been known as the **Raymond Knight Stampede Grounds**.

Hometown Hockey Hero

The arena named for Maurice "The Rocket" Richard (1921–2000), the most famous player in Montreal Canadiens' history, is a 4,750-seat facility situated very close to Olympic Stadium, the massive former home of the Montreal Expos.

HOMETOWN TRIBUTE:

Aréna Maurice-Richard, Montreal, Quebec.

From Defence to Doughnuts

Hard to believe now, but before 1964 the name Tim Horton had nothing to do with double-doubles, drive-throughs, or doughnuts. Back then, Tim Horton was just a modestly famous 34-year-old hockey player. His Toronto Maple Leafs had just won the Stanley Cup three years in a row.

But Horton had also been dabbling in business off the ice. Previous ventures – a hamburger restaurant, a car dealership – had done okay. But then in 1964, Horton and his business partner hit upon the idea of opening a "doughnut shop" in Hamilton, Ontario. They figured that by putting the Tim Horton name on the sign out front, hockey fans would be sure to show up in droves. And Hamilton had a lot of hockey fans. From that humble start, Tim Hortons has grown to be the most successful restaurant chain in Canada, with more than 3,300 locations across the country today.

So, in a way, Tim Horton has more places named for him than any other Canadian sports personality past or present. But there is at least one site named for Horton that still has nothing to do with double-doubles, drive-throughs, or doughnuts. **The Tim Hortons Events Centre** opened in 2006 in the northern city of Cochrane, Ontario, where the future Maple Leafs defenseman lived until he was 15. Hometowns never forget their famous sons and daughters.

Sports Pages

Don't forget that fishing is a real sport, too. And if sport fishing's your game, why not check out the writings of Roderick Haig-Brown, an Englishman who visited Canada in the 1930s and loved the country so much that he spent much of the rest of his life tracking salmon in rivers around Vancouver Island and writing about his experiences.

His essays on sport fishing such as *A River Never Sleeps* and *Measure of the Year* are a good place to start, and his *A Primer of Fly Fishing* is considered a standard work on the subject. Haig-Brown's novel for kids, *Saltwater Summer*, is based on his adventures salmon fishing off the extreme western edge of the country.

The British Columbia government thought so much of Haig-Brown's efforts to preserve salmon habitats that it named **Roderick Haig-Brown Provincial Park** in his honour in 1977. The University of Victoria, where Haig-Brown was chancellor, has likewise named **R. Haig-Brown Hall** as a tribute.

Tru-Story

By longstanding tradition, many Canadian prime ministers have attended a Grey Cup game. Which Canadian leader attended the most Grey Cups? Canada's 15th prime minister, Pierre Elliott Trudeau, showed up at a record seven Grey Cup games between 1968 and 1981.

The PM turned a lot of heads with his outlandish fashion choices at the 1970 championship game, as seen in a classic Canadian Press photo. Arriving in style to present the trophy to the victorious Montreal Alouettes, the smiling Trudeau sported plaid pants, a beige jacket with a rose in the lapel, and a tilted Havana chapeau. Best of all, note the superman-style cape!

Places named after Pierre Elliott Trudeau:

- Pierre Elliott Trudeau Park, Côte Saint-Luc, Quebec
- Pierre Elliott Trudeau Park, Vaughan, Ontario
- Pierre Elliott Trudeau Mountain, Valemount, British Columbia
- Pierre Elliott Trudeau Airport, Montreal, Quebec
- Rue Pierre-E-Trudeau, Montreal, Quebec
- Pierre Elliott Trudeau Public School, Oshawa, Ontario
- College Pierre Elliott Trudeau, Winnipeg, Manitoba

- Pierre Elliott Trudeau Elementary School, Vancouver, British Columbia
- École Pierre-Elliott-Trudeau, Nepean, Ontario
- École Pierre-Elliott-Trudeau, Toronto, Ontario
- Pierre Elliott Trudeau High School, Markham, Ontario
- Pierre Elliott Trudeau School, Vaudreuil-Dorion, Quebec
- Pierre Elliott Trudeau School, Gatineau, Quebec

Hometown Hockey Hero

Pete Morin's NHL career lasted a mere 31 games. In 1941–42, his only year with the Montreal Canadiens, Morin (1915–2000) hit double digits in goals and recorded 22 points. He played another decade in a provincial senior league before retiring.

HOMETOWN TRIBUTE:

Aréna Pierre Morin, Montreal, Quebec.

Polo Pioneer

The printed record of everything politicians say in Canada's House of Commons is called the Hansard. According to Hansard, on September 27, 2001, Ontario MP Bryon Wilfert rose in the House to "announce the official opening of **Phyllis Rawlinson Park** in my riding of Oak Ridges. Phyllis Rawlinson, an artist, naval officer, polo player, farmer, horsewoman, and all-round dynamic individual passed away in 1995. She bequeathed the 90-acre property to the town of Richmond Hill on the understanding that it would be used as a park …"

Little else is widely known about the polo-playing Ms. Rawlinson, who lived quietly on a farm outside Richmond Hill for most of her life. The Empire Club of Canada has noted that she was "one of the four women polo players to play competitively internationally for Canada in the 1930s and served with the British Wrens trained by Billy Bishop throughout World War II."

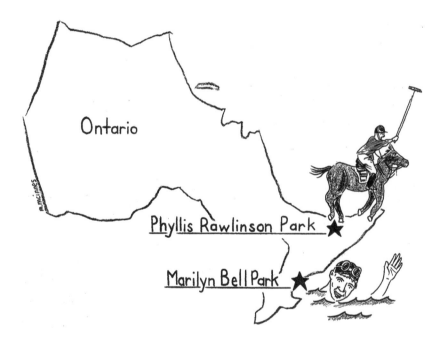

Like Great-Grandfather, Like Great-Grandson

Every hockeyphile should check out the cover of Peter Gzowski's book *The Game of Our Lives*. It captures a perfect hockey moment. The picture, taken from high above the ice during a game, shows Wayne Gretzky of the Edmonton Oilers five feet from the net, the puck on his stick, while Colorado Rockies goalie Chico Resch makes a desperate sprawling attempt to stop yet another Gretzky goal.

Turn the cover and you'll find Peter Gzowski's true account of the 1980–81 season, which he spent travelling around the NHL with the upstart Edmonton Oilers. With a roster that included a bunch of future Hall of Famers, the team was on the verge of Stanley Cup greatness.

Gzowski was a well-known broadcaster and writer who died in 2002. He also happened to be the great-grandson of Sir Casimir Gzowski, the Polish aristocrat who moved to Canada, designed the Welland Canal, and is the namesake of Toronto's **Sir Casimir Gzowski Park**. Not to be outdone by his famous ancestor, Peter is also honoured with the naming of a Canadian place – two, in fact. **The Peter Gzowski Amphitheatre** at the Cambridge Centre for the Arts was officially named in September of 2002. Trent University, where Gzowski was chancellor, named its **Peter Gzowski College** after him in 2003.

Hometown Hockey Hero

On October 9, 1974, in a game against the Toronto Maple Leafs, Simon Nolet scored the first-ever goal for the short-lived Kansas City Scouts of the NHL. Nolet was born in 1941 in the tiny Quebec village of Saint-Odilon-de-Cranbourne near the town of Lac-Etchemin.

HOMETOWN TRIBUTE:

Aréna Simon Nolet, Lac-Etchemin, Quebec.

Recovering Their Heart and Soles

When Toronto's **Percy Williams Junior Public School** opened on November 17, 1983, it was given a piece of Canadian history to celebrate the occasion: a pair of Percy Williams's shoes. The important track and field relics were the shoes Williams wore when he set the world record for the 100-metre sprint at the 1930 British Empire Games.

On the morning of March 18, 2005, staff and students were shocked to find their treasured possession gone. During the night, thieves had broken into the school by smashing through a rear door window. No computers were taken. No money was stolen from the school office. The only item missing was the school's most guarded prize, Williams's shoes, which had been stored in a locked display case.

Luckily, sleuths from the Toronto police detective squad soon got a tip from the public and were able to restore the famous footwear to its special glass case four days later.

An eerily similar episode 25 years earlier did not have such a happy ending, however. Back in January of 1980, the two gold medals Percy Williams won at the 1928 Olympics were ripped from their permanent displays at the B.C. Sports Hall of Fame, never to be recovered. Speculation at the time was that the perpetrators of this cowardly crime — no one was ever arrested — had pilfered the medals so they could be melted down and traded for cash on the gold market.

Sneaker Power

The Converse Jack Purcell sneaker is one of the best-selling shoe brands in history. Canadian badminton champion John Edward "Jack" Purcell designed the shoe for the BF Goodrich Company in 1935 because he felt regular running shoes didn't provide enough support and protection on badminton courts. Not to mention most shoes were kind of ugly. Converse has owned the rights to the shoe since 1970. By the way, Jack was successful with his new fashionable footwear: he remained badminton's world champion until his retirement in 1945. **Jack Purcell Community Centre** in Ottawa, Ontario, commemorates this amazing athlete. You'll find it at 320 **Jack Purcell Lane**.

Two Olympians in One

After a few laps around Winnipeg's **Susan Auch Speed Skating Oval,** named for Olympic medal-winning speed skater Susan Auch, you won't have to go far to find another facility named for a great Canadian Olympian. The oval is *inside* the **Cindy Klassen Recreation Complex**, which takes its name from Canada's most decorated Olympian of all time.

Sports Pages

James Naismith, whose name is found on street signs in Ottawa and Almonte, Ontario, wrote the very first document of any kind about basketball — way back in 1892. Naismith's "13 Rules of Basket Ball" (note *basketball* is still two separate words) appeared in the Springfield College school newspaper *The Triangle* on January 15 of that year.

Tribute to a Hockey Dad

Why did Archie Courtnall, father of two NHL sons, commit suicide in 1978? Pondering that question, the writer of a 1997 *New York Daily News* article guessed that it must have been because of "the frustration of a stunted hockey career that reached Cleveland of the American Hockey League" and his dismal post-hockey job "scaling logs at a wood mill."

More likely, the former Cleveland Barons forward suffered from a mental illness that doctors could have treated with improved methods. With their dad in mind, Archie's sons Geoff and Russ Courtnall — Geoff played more than 1,000 NHL career games and Russ was a star player with the Toronto Maple Leafs and Vancouver Canucks — helped the Royal Jubilee Hospital in Victoria, British Columbia, raise money to add a new section in 2004. Named the **Archie Courtnall Centre**, the facility is "designed to provide psychiatric assessment, stabilization and intervention" for patients with mental health issues.

Hometown Hockey Hero

During their Stanley Cup run of 1938, the Chicago Black Hawks called up minor leaguer Pete Palangio from St. Louis of the American Hockey Association. Pete was in the lineup when the Hawks won the championship that year. He died in 2004 at the age of 96.

HOMETOWN TRIBUTE:

Pete Palangio Arena, North Bay, Ontario.

Best-of-One

Tom Brook Athletic Park in Calgary, Alberta, commemorates a man who preserved a Canadian sports tradition.

The Grey Cup is the annual championship game of the Canadian Football League, played each year since 1909. But in 1949, it was on the verge of being radically changed. Many team bosses wanted to change the game's format, turning it into a best-of-three series similar to the NHL hockey playoffs. According to stories, it was Tom Brook, then owner of the Calgary Stampeders, who finally persuaded everyone to stick to the single-game event Canadian football fans were used to.

Thomas McQuesten

Residents of Hamilton, Ontario, are familiar with the name Thomas McQuesten. One of city's most travelled roadways is called the **Thomas McQuesten Bridge** and a popular sports venue there is called **T.B. McQuesten Park.**

McQuesten is known as the provincial politician who, as Minister of Highways, helped create the Queen Elizabeth Way, the Rainbow Bridge, and lots of other important construction projects. He was minister until 1943.

But before deciding on politics as a career, McQuesten was on course for a remarkable pro sports career. As a teenager, McQuesten had helped the Hamilton Collegiate Institute win a high-school championship in 1900. He soon caught on with a professional team. Although records from the time are vague, he was definitely a member of the Hamilton Tigers football club, now the Hamilton Tiger-Cats. In 1908, the Tigers won the Dominion Championship, the forerunner of the Grey Cup. McQuesten even briefly joined the Toronto Argonauts while he was a student at the University of Toronto.

Sports Pages

Olympic figure skating silver medalist at the 1988 games, Elizabeth Manley — namesake of **The Elizabeth Manley Rink** in Ottawa, Ontario — has produced two books about her life. With co-writers, Manley published *Thumbs Up!: The Elizabeth Manley Story* in 1990 and *As I Am: My Life After the Olympics* in 1999.

Lueders Loop

Next time life throws you for a loop, cheer up by recalling what happened to Canadian bobsledder Pierre Lueders in 2008. That March, Lueders was piloting his sled down the icy twists and turns of the Whistler Sliding Centre in British Columbia. As the former world champion sledder approached the sharp 180-degree turn in Corner 7 of the course, something went wrong. Lueders, still unfamiliar with the newly built layout of the Sliding Centre, appeared to lose control. Suddenly, Bam! As observers watched helplessly, Lueders crashed violently into the hairpin turn at a speed of close to 150 kilometres per hour. Fortunately, Lueders was able to dust himself off after the wipeout and was none the worse for wear. When all was said and done, Lueders even got a tiny but permanent part of Canada named after him. Corner 7 at the Whistler Sliding Centre is now known as **Lueders Loop**.

The Mike Richards Way

The year 2010 was eventful for Kenora, Ontario, native Mike Richards. The Philadelphia Flyers captain scored his 100th NHL goal in February that year and then surprised the hockey world by leading the 8th place Flyers to an appearance in the Stanley Cup Finals. That winter, Richards was selected to play for Canada at the Olympic Games in Vancouver, where he helped his country win gold in front of the home crowd.

The people of Kenora were so proud of Mike that, before the summer was out, they named a street after him. Kenora bylaw 135-2010 reads in part "… in order to indicate the City's pride in one of its own … Council deems it expedient to rename the street leading into the Kenora Recreation Centre as **Mike Richards Way.**"

The Man in the Photograph

There is a famous photograph of Percy Williams taken after the runner had won gold for Canada in the 100-metre sprint at the 1928 Amsterdam Olympics. In the picture, the skinny Vancouverite is triumphantly carried on the shoulders of two unidentified athletes, one of whom was in fact substitute runner Harry Warren. Warren, who died in 1998, is the namesake of **Harry Warren Field** at the University of British Columbia in Richmond, British Columbia.

Somewhat overshadowed by Percy Williams, Warren's own athletic high point happened at the 1928 Irish Games, where he captured first place in the 100-metre dash. Back in Canada, Warren set about persuading Canadians to embrace a type of hockey they were mostly unfamiliar with – field hockey. The sport quickly jumped in popularity. This brainy sportsman was a professor, too. At the University of British Columbia, Warren was a pioneer in a field with a really long name: biogeochemistry. He could predict with uncanny accuracy the minerals in soil by looking at the plants on the surface.

Terry Fox

Terry Fox's inspiring cross-country run to raise money to help find a cure for cancer took place in 1980. With one leg already amputated, Fox began his Marathon of Hope in Newfoundland in April. He made it all the way to Thunder Bay, Ontario, before calling off the run when his disease worsened in September. The Marathon of Hope wasn't technically a sport, but running the equivalent of a marathon every day for five months puts Fox on par with any athlete.

At least 27 Canadian places are named after Terry Fox:

- Terry Fox Elementary School, Abbotsford, British Columbia
- Terry Fox Elementary School, Barrie, Ontario
- Terry Fox Elementary School, Pierrefonds, Quebec
- Terry Fox Junior High School, Calgary, Alberta
- Terry Fox Elementary School, Newmarket, Ontario
- Terry Fox Elementary School, Bathurst, New Brunswick
- Terry Fox Secondary School, Port Coquitlam, British Columbia
- Terry Fox Theatre, Port Coquitlam, British Columbia
- The Terry Fox Library, Port Coquitlam, British Columbia
- Terry Fox Drive, Ottawa, Ontario
- Terry Fox Drive, Kingston, Ontario
- Terry Fox Way, Mississauga, Ontario
- Terry Fox Way, Vancouver, British Columbia
- Terry Fox Boulevard, Saint-Eustache, Quebec
- Rue Terry Fox, Mascouche, Quebec
- Terry Fox Courage Highway, Thunder Bay, Ontario
- Terry Fox Field, Simon Fraser University, Burnaby, British Columbia
- The Terry Fox Trail, St. Catharines, Ontario
- Terry Fox Track, Saskatoon, Saskatchewan
- The Track and Field Stadium, Brampton, Ontario
- Terry Fox Gymnasium, Brighton, Ontario
- Terry Fox Drive, Brighton, Ontario
- Terry Fox Place, Sault Ste. Marie, Ontario
- The Terry Fox Youth Centre, Ottawa, Ontario
- Terry Fox Memorial Pool, Mississauga, Ontario
- The Terry Fox Sports Complex, Sudbury, Ontario
- Mount Terry Fox, Valemount, British Columbia

Hometown Hockey Hero

A dependable defensive player, Jean-Guy Talbot (1932–) was a member of Stanley Cup–winning Montreal Canadiens teams in the late 1950s. He was traded to the Minnesota North Stars in 1967. As head coach of the New York Rangers in the 1970s, Talbot often wore a track suit instead of a suit and tie as he stood behind the bench during games.

HOMETOWN TRIBUTE:

Aréna Jean-Guy Talbot, Cap-de-la-Madeleine, Quebec (now part of Trois Rivières).

Political Syl

Syl Apps played centre for the Toronto Maple Leafs from 1936 to 1948. During the 1940 season, a federal election was held in Canada. Even though he was just 25 years old and the Leafs were in the middle of a Stanley Cup playoff run, Syl decided to run as a candidate for the National Government Party in the election. When all the votes were counted, Syl had lost by only 138 votes. For the Leafs it was a good thing Syl didn't get that new job in parliament: he led them to a Stanley Cup win in 1942.

After hockey, Syl did become a politician in Ontario. He was also inducted into the Hockey Hall of Fame. At least three Ontario places recognize his remarkable career: the **Syl Apps Youth Centre** in Oakville, the **Syl Apps Community Centre** in Paris, and the **Syl and Molly Apps Research Centre** in Kingston.

Foreign Affairs

When auto racing events are held at the Zolder Circuit in Belgium, you are likely to see flowers placed beside the part of the track now called Villeneuve Corner. Race fans will always remember Zolder as the place where legendary Canadian racer Gilles Villeneuve died in a crash of his Ferrari during a qualifying lap of the Belgian Grand Prix on May 8, 1982. In Italy, where Villeneuve enjoyed great popularity in his career, **Villeneuve Corner** at the Autodromo Enzo e Dino Ferrari race track, former site of the San Marino Grand Prix, also memorializes the Villeneuve name.

Parking Spaces

Here's a page that really knocks it out of the park. Walk past any place on the list below and you might see a ballgame underway, dogs fetching tennis balls, or kids tossing a Frisbee around. Each bears the name of an outstanding athletic Canuck. So park yourself someplace comfortable and give it a read.

- Mike Weir Park, Sarnia, Ontario (golf)
- Billy Sherring Park, Hamilton, Ontario (track and field)
- Marilyn Bell Park, Toronto, Ontario (swimming)
- Dannie Seaman Park, Liverpool, Nova Scotia (baseball)
- Bobbie Rosenfeld Park, Toronto, Ontario (multi-sport)
- Emery Barnes Park, Vancouver, British Columbia (football)
- George Vernot Park, Montreal, Quebec (swimming)
- Susan Auch Park, Winnipeg, Manitoba (speed skating)

- Elizabeth Manley Park, Ottawa, Ontario (figure skating)
- Jim Waite Park, St. Thomas, Ontario (curling)
- Paul Landry Park, Ottawa, Ontario (track and field)
- Fergie Jenkins Park, Chatham, Ontario (baseball)
- Sir Casimir Gzowski Park, Toronto, Ontario (horse racing)
- Sandra Schmirler Olympic Gold Park, Biggar, Saskatchewan (curling)
- Phyllis Rawlinson Park, Richmond Hill, Ontario (polo)
- Tom Brook Athletic Park, Calgary, Alberta (football)
- Thomas McQuesten Park, Hamilton, Ontario (football)
- Sue Holloway Fitness Park, Ottawa, Ontario (skiing)
- Alan Wilson Park, Duncan, British Columbia (football)
- Donovan Bailey Park, Oakville, Ontario (track and field)
- Bobby Kerr Park, Hamilton, Ontario (football)
- Dave King Park, Saskatoon, Saskatchewan (hockey/coaching)
- Marita Payne Park, Vaughan, Ontario (track and field)
- Johnny Bright Sports Park, Edmonton, Alberta (football)
- Jack Purcell Park, Ottawa, Ontario (badminton)
- Terry Sawchuk Memorial Park, Winnipeg, Manitoba (hockey)
- Parc Gilles-Villeneuve, Berthierville, Quebec (auto racing)

Swimming in Saskatoon

"Hall of Fame Swimmer Dies" announced the CBC online news headline when Harry Bailey died in April of 2000. A member of the Saskatchewan Sports Hall of Fame, Bailey was a provincial breast stroke champion in the 1930s, setting records he would hold well into the 1940s.

Before Bailey, few had ever heard the word *aquacade*, the swimming equivalent of an air show. After retiring from competition, Bailey was the organizer behind the first of these events in Saskatoon, which quickly became popular. In 1977, the people of Saskatoon recognized his lifelong love of swimming by naming the **Harry Bailey Aquatic Centre** in his honour.

Super Hooper

At a ceremony on June 24, 2005, the Colonnade Soccer Fields in Nepean, Ontario, were officially renamed the **Charmaine Hooper Soccer Fields**. When she retired from the national team in 2006, Hooper had made 129 appearances for Canada and scored 71 goals, both national records at the time. Born in a seaside South American city in 1968, Hooper came to Canada as a child and quickly took soccer leagues around Ottawa by storm. As a pro, when she wasn't playing for the Canadian national team, Hooper enjoyed stints with the Atlanta Beat, the Rockford Dactyls, the Chicago Cobras, and the New Jersey Wildcats of the Women's United Soccer Association.

A Canadian Olympic First

Hayley Wickenheiser, one of the best women's hockey players in the world, played on Canada's women's hockey team at the Olympic Games in 1998, 2002, 2006, and 2010. When she suited up with the Canadian women's softball team at the 2000 Summer Olympics in Sydney, Australia, she became the second woman to represent Canada at both the Summer and Winter Olympic Games. Who was the first?

That distinction belongs to Sue Holloway. She became the first Canadian, male or female, to manage the feat when she took part in cross-country skiing at the 1976 Winter Games in Austria and then canoe sprint at the 1976 Summer Olympics in Montreal. This amazing Canadian first is commemorated with the **Sue Holloway Fitness Park** in Ottawa, Ontario.

The Best Road They Could Name

"The Hockey Song" by Canadian folk singer Stompin' Tom Connors is often played at NHL arenas during games, to the delight of those in attendance. The tune's easy-to-sing-along-with lyrics are known by legions of hockey fans who no doubt agree with Stompin' Tom that the best game you can name is, well, the good ol' hockey game.

Can't make it to a game? Give the track a listen on YouTube, or better yet, find the original on Tom's fittingly named 1973 album *Stompin Tom' and The Hockey Song*. Come to think of it, the best way to hear the song may well be from a car stereo as you cruise down **Stompin' Tom Road** in the scenic village of Skinners Pond, Prince Edward Island. The people of Tom's boyhood community proudly named the road after him in 1999.

Sports Pages

Jacques Plante — namesake of **Jacques Plante Arena** in Shawinigan, Quebec, and the first NHL goalie to regularly wear a face mask — wrote a very successful book for aspiring netminders. Simply titled *Goaltending*, it was published in 1972. By popular demand, it was reprinted in 1997.

The Devil's in the Details

What if the word for the Devil's hangout wasn't spelled "H-E-Double Hockey Sticks," but "H-E-Double Curling Brooms" instead?

W.O. Mitchell's play *The Black Bonspiel of Wullie MacCrimmon* is the tale of shoemaker and part-time curler Wullie MacCrimmon and his dream of winning Canada's biggest curling tournament, The Brier.

In the play, the Devil passes through the small town of Wildrose, Alberta, and offers to deliver Wullie the win. In return, Wullie must sell his soul — and forever play for the Devil's curling team in Hell. At first Wullie accepts, but he soon realizes the terrible mistake he has made. It all comes down to a winner-take-all showdown between Wullie's team, made up of himself and his three best buddies, against the Devil's rink, including Macbeth, Judas Iscariot, and Guy Fawkes.

Note to students at **W.O. Mitchell Elementary School** in Kanata, Ontario, and **W.O. Mitchell Elementary School** in Calgary, Alberta: Make sure your school library has a copy of this play!

Hometown Hockey Heroes: Part Two

Like the other Hockey Heroes in this book, the players discussed below have places named after them back home. Many are in Quebec and Ontario. Those who lace up their skates in these arenas can draw extra inspiration from the illustrious hockey names emblazoned on the sign out front.

Mark Messier (1961–) scored 19 hat tricks in his 25-year NHL career, and is currently second on the all-time career points list. Only Wayne Gretzky, his former Edmonton Oilers teammate, has more. The hardnosed winger won five Stanley Cups — four with the Oilers and one with the New York Rangers. He obtained Hall of Fame membership in 2007. **Hometown tribute:** Mark Messier Rink, St. Albert, Alberta.

Dave Keon (1940–) captained the Toronto Maple Leafs squad that won the 1967 Stanley Cup. Only Mats Sundin ranks above Keon in all-time Leafs scoring. An enigmatic figure, Keon has rarely been seen by fans since his retirement. He ended his Hall of Fame career in 1982 with the Hartford Whalers. **Hometown tribute:** Aréna Dave Keon, Rouyn-Noranda, Quebec.

André Lacroix (1945–) was a point-scoring machine for several World Hockey Association teams in the 1970s. He played well during his NHL year, as well, leading the Philadelphia Flyers in scoring at the end of the 1960s and at the beginning of the 1970s. **Hometown tribute:** Aréna André Lacroix, Lévis, Quebec.

High-scoring **Mike Bossy** (1957–) played ten NHL seasons, all with New York Islanders. He was a key member of the Islanders teams that won four consecutive Stanley Cups from 1980 to 1983. **Hometown tribute:** Aréna Mike-Bossy, Laval, Quebec.

Jacques Laperrière (1941–), a standout Montreal Canadiens defenceman who won six Stanley Cups as a player, was born in the Quebec town of Rouyn before it merged with the former town of Noranda. The arena named for Laperrière is nestled in the historic Rouyn section of town. **Hometown tribute:** Aréna Jacques Laperrière, Rouyn-Noranda, Quebec.

Even true hockey aficionados sometimes lose track of the long list of Montreal Canadiens greats. Folks familiar with "Rocket" Richard, Guy Lafleur, and Jean Béliveau should take another look at the remarkable career of **Claude Larose** (1943–) who won six Stanley Cups with Montreal between 1965 and 1973. Larose hails from Hearst, a largely francophone northern Ontario community. **Hometown tribute:** Claude Larose Arena, Hearst, Ontario.

Reggie Lemelin (1954–), along with Mike Vernon and Miikka Kiprusoff, is arguably among the best goalies in Calgary Flames history. He was with the team from 1980 to 1987. Before retiring, Lemelin took his goaltending skills to the Boston Bruins, with whom he won the Jennings Trophy (for fewest goals allowed) with Andy Moog in 1990. **Hometown tribute:** Aréna Réjean-Lemelin, Charlesbourg, Quebec.

Gilles Lupien (1954–), a popular but low-scoring defenceman, was a member of the Montreal Canadiens teams that won the Stanley Cup in 1978 and 1979. Lupien, a native of Brownsburg, Quebec, also played for the Pittsburgh Penguins and Hartford Whalers. **Hometown tribute:** Aréna Gilles Lupien, Brownsburg, Quebec.

Howie Morenz (1902–37) played part of his career with the Rangers and the Black Hawks but is remembered best as a Montreal Canadien. His death at age 34 from complications that arose due to a leg injury suffered in a game against the Chicago Black Hawks shocked the hockey world. He remains an admired figure from the early days of twentieth-century hockey. **Hometown tribute:** Aréna Howie-Morenz, Montreal, Quebec.

Pat Quinn (1943–) played nine NHL seasons on defence for the Toronto Maple Leafs, Vancouver Canucks, and Atlanta Flames. Retiring before the 1978 season, Quinn began a highly successful coaching career, taking his squads – including Mats Sundin and the early 2000s Maple Leafs – to the playoffs 15 times. Quinn also coached Team Canada to a gold medal at the 2002 Olympics in Salt Lake City. **Hometown tribute:** Pat Quinn Parkdale Arena, Hamilton, Ontario.

Along with other now-retired players like Dave Andreychuk and Luc Robitaille, **Stéphane Richer** (1966–) was among the best left wingers active in the NHL during the early 1990s. A two-time Stanley Cup winner, Richer scored 421 career goals. **Hometown tribute:** Aréna Stéphane Richer, Saint-André-Avellin, Quebec.

Goaltender **Frank McCool** (1918–73) won the Calder Trophy for best rookie in 1945. That year with the Toronto Maple Leafs he recorded four playoff shutouts, three of them in consecutive games against the Detroit Red Wings. Sadly, severe stomach ulcers limited McCool's career to just two NHL seasons. The ice rink named for McCool officially opened January 17, 1976. **Hometown tribute:** Frank McCool Arena, Calgary, Alberta.

You Can Call Me Al

His nickname may have been "Dirt," but Al Wilson had a near-spotless record during his 15 years as an all-star lineman with the BC Lions of the Canadian Football League from 1972 to 1986. He once put together an "iron man" streak of 167 consecutive games played. He's now a member of both the CFL Hall of Fame and the BC Lions Hall of Fame.

The people of Duncan, British Columbia, are proud of Wilson, and have named two places in their town for him, **Alan Wilson Park** and **Al Wilson Grove**.

Wilson has lived in British Columbia all his life, except during his college years when he attended Montana State University (MSU). Al brought good luck to MSU: the year he arrived on campus, the school's archeologists dug up – out of the "dirt" around Billings – the largest Tyrannosaurus Rex skull ever found.

"The Jackie Robinson of Hockey"

Jackie Robinson of the Brooklyn Dodgers famously broke baseball's colour barrier on April 15, 1947. That day he gained immortality by becoming the first black Major League Baseball player. More than ten years later, an equivalent milestone was finally achieved in hockey.

When Willie O'Ree of the Boston Bruins stepped onto the ice in a game against the Montreal Canadiens on January 8, 1958, he became the first black player in the history of the NHL. The New Brunswick–born O'Ree scored 14 points with the Bruins over two NHL seasons and won two scoring titles in the minor leagues during his long hockey career. He retired in 1979 as a member of the San Diego Hawks of the Pacific Hockey League.

Willie O'Ree Place, a sports complex in O'Ree's hometown of Fredericton, New Brunswick, was officially opened in a special ceremony attended by O'Ree on January 16, 2008 – exactly 50 years and eight days after his historic NHL debut.

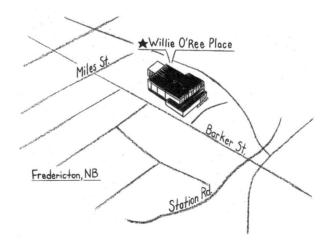

Sports Pages

In the 1930s, Herb Carnegie was one of few black hockey players in Canada. Today his name is emblazoned on the front of the **Herbert H. Carnegie Centennial Centre** in Toronto. Although he never made it to the NHL, Carnegie played several seasons with the Quebec Aces in the Quebec Senior League and was once offered a minor league contract with the New York Rangers. You can read about his interesting life in the 1997 book he co-wrote titled *A Fly in a Pail of Milk: The Herb Carnegie Story.*

Into the Wild

William Dickenson Hunter was better known to everybody in the hockey world simply as "Wild Bill." He's best known for being the GM and coach of the Edmonton Oilers in the years just before the team acquired Wayne Gretzky and joined the NHL. His later efforts to get an NHL team for the city of Saskatoon – he came close but a deal never panned out – are also fondly remembered by many western Canadians.

Bill had a temper. According to stories, he got his nickname after a fiery dispute with a referee during one of his many coaching jobs in 1940s Saskatchewan.

After Bill died, two Canadian spaces were named after him as a tribute to his 65 years in sports: **Bill Hunter Arena** in Edmonton and **Bill Hunter Avenue** in Saskatoon. Some say the names are a little "tamer" than Bill might have liked. Both leave off the "Wild" from his name.

Sports Pages

Even though "Wild" Bill Hunter came up short trying to bring an NHL team to Saskatoon, grateful Saskatonians rewarded him anyway with the naming of **Bill Hunter Avenue** in their city. Read all about Hunter's roller-coaster career in the autobiography he co-wrote in 2000 called *Wild Bill: Bill Hunter's Legendary 65 Years in Canadian Sport.* The foreword is by Wayne Gretzky.

Pat Burns, Coach

The official ceremony held to announce the naming of **Pat Burns Arena** took place in Stanstead, Quebec, on March 26, 2010. (Burns, who won 501 games in his coaching career, is one of only three Boston Bruins coaches to win the Jack Adams Award for coach of the year – Claude Julien and "Coach's Corner" star Don Cherry are the others.) The guest list at the ceremony that day included prime minister Stephen Harper, Canadian senator Jacques Demers, and a number of current NHL players such as New Jersey Devils goalie Martin Brodeur and former players such as onetime Maple Leafs netminder Felix Potvin.

Also attending was a group of Quebec minor hockey players. Despite battling advanced cancer, Burns took the podium at the event held in his honour and had a few special words for those young players. "Maybe there's a Wayne Gretzky or a Mario Lemieux or a Sidney Crosby sitting here," he said. With an eye to the future, the coach added prophetically: "A young player could [one day] come from Stanstead who plays in an arena named after me."

The Greatest Portrait

It's one of the most memorable portraits anywhere of the legendary boxer Muhammad Ali. The three-time world heavyweight champion, standing against a stark black background and wearing a pinstripe suit instead of his usual boxing trunks and gloves, glares at the camera, his hands posed defiantly on his hips. This is one tough customer who won't go down without a fight.

This special photograph of Ali, whose nickname was "The Greatest," was taken by a Canadian, the renowned portrait photographer Yousuf Karsh, in a New York studio in 1970. It's been displayed in various places, but it took 35 years to find it the perfect home. Today it can be seen on a wall of the **Estrellita and Yousuf Karsh Emergency Department** at the Children's Hospital in Ottawa – officially named in honour of Karsh and his wife on September 21, 2005 – where it offers quiet inspiration to kids fighting their own battles against serious illness.

Sports Pages

Nancy Greene, medal-winning Olympic skier and namesake of British Columbia's **Nancy Greene Provincial Park**, has authored two books. *Nancy Greene: An Autobiography*, written with Jack Batten, was published in 1968. Her book *Alpine Skiing* came out in 1975.

Parallel Lives

In September of 2001, the University of British Columbia (UBC) officially named one of its sports fields after respected former athlete and sports administrator Harry Wright. It isn't the only field at UBC named for a Harold. Check out the eerie points of similarity between these two Harrys. (You can't make this stuff up.)

Harold "Harry" Warren (born 1904)	Harold "Harry" Wright (born 1908)
Has a field named after him at UBC. (Harry Warren Field)	Has a field named after him at UBC. (Harold Wright Field)
Initials: H.W.	Initials: H.W.
Earned geology degree from University of British Columbia	Earned geology degree from University of British Columbia
Member of Canadian track and field team, 1928 Amsterdam Olympics	Member of Canadian track and field team, 1932 Los Angeles Olympics
Knew legendary Canadian sprinter Percy Williams	Knew Percy Williams
Past President, Canadian Field Hockey Association	Past President, Canadian Field Hockey Association

Appendix A

At the Olympics

Many athletes honoured with Canadian place names have represented Canada at the Olympic Games. This list shows how they did and which Canadian places are named for them.

Syl Apps
Places:
> Syl Apps Youth Centre, Oakville, Ontario
> Syl Apps Community Centre, Paris, Ontario
> Syl and Molly Apps Research Centre, Kingston, Ontario

Olympic record:
> 6th place, pole vault, 1936, Berlin, Germany

Susan Auch
Places:
> Susan Auch Park, Winnipeg, Manitoba
> Susan Auch Speed Skating Oval, Winnipeg, Manitoba

Olympic record:
> Bronze medal, speed skating, 3,000-metre relay, 1988, Calgary, Canada
> Silver medal, speed skating, 500-metre, 1994, Lillehammer, Norway
> Silver medal, speed skating, 500-metre, 1998, Nagano, Japan

Donovan Bailey

Places:

Donovan Bailey Park, Oakville, Ontario

Olympic record:

Gold medal, track and field, 100-metre, 1996, Atlanta, United States

Gold medal, track and field, 4x100-metre relay, 1996, Atlanta

Member of Canadian track and field team, 2000, Sydney, Australia

Emery Barnes

Places:

Emery Barnes Park, Vancouver, British Columbia

Olympic record:

Member of United States track and field team, high jump, 1952, Helsinki, Finland

Hilton Belyea

Places:

Hilton Belyea Arena, Saint John, New Brunswick

Olympic record:

Awarded special bronze medal for sportsmanship, rowing, men's single sculls, 1924, Paris, France

Kurt Browning

Places:

Kurt Browning Arena, Caroline, Alberta

Olympic record:

8th place, men's figure skating, 1988, Calgary

6th place, men's figure skating, 1992, Albertville, France

5th place, men's figure skating, 1994, Lillehammer

Eric Coy

Places:

Eric Coy Arena, Winnipeg, Manitoba

Eric Coy District, Winnipeg, Manitoba

Olympic record:

23rd place, track and field, discus throw, 1948, London, England

Clarence Downey

Places:

Clarence Downey Speed Skating Oval, Saskatoon, Saskatchewan

Olympic record:

Coach, Canadian speed skating team, 1956, Melbourne, Australia

Charles Gorman

Places:

Charles Gorman Arena, Saint John, New Brunswick

Olympic record:

7th place, speed skating, 500-metre, 1924, Chamonix, France

11th place, speed skating, 1,500-metre, 1924, Chamonix

7th place, speed skating, 500-metre, 1928, St. Moritz, Switzerland

12th place, speed skating, 1,500-metre, 1928, St. Moritz

Nancy Greene

Places:

Nancy Greene Provincial Park, near Castlegar, British Columbia

Nancy Greene Lake, Monashee Mountains, Kootenay Region, British Columbia

Olympic record:

Member of Canadian ski team, 1960, Squaw Valley, California, United States

Member of Canadian ski team, 1964, Innsbruck, Austria

Gold medal, skiing, giant slalom (GS), 1968, Grenoble, France

Silver medal, skiing, slalom, 1968, Grenoble

Wayne Gretzky

Places:

Wayne Gretzky Parkway, Brantford, Ontario

Wayne Gretzky Sports Centre, Brantford, Ontario

Wayne Gretzky Way, Edmonton, Alberta

Olympic record:

4th place, men's ice hockey, 1998, Nagano

Sue Holloway

Places:

Sue Holloway Fitness Park, Ottawa, Ontario

Olympic record:

7th place, 4x5-kilometre cross-country skiing relay, 1976, Innsbruck*

32nd place, 10-kilometre women's cross-country skiing, 1976, Innsbruck

Member of Canadian Olympic Team, women's canoe sprint, 1976, Montreal, Canada*

Silver medal, women's canoe sprint, K-2 500-metre, 1984, Los Angeles, United States

Bronze medal, women's canoe sprint, K-4 500-metre, 1984, Los Angeles

*First Canadian to compete in both Summer and Winter Games in the same year

Harry Jerome

Places:

Harry Jerome Sports Centre, Burnaby, British Columbia

Harry Jerome Track, Prince Albert, Saskatchewan

Harry Jerome Sports Complex, Vancouver

Harry Jerome Weight Room, University of Oregon

Olympic record:

Bronze medal, track and field, 100-metre, 1964, Tokyo, Japan

Joé Juneau

Places:

Aréna Joé-Juneau, Pont-Rouge, Quebec

Olympic record:

Silver medal, men's ice hockey, 1992, Albertville

Bobby Kerr

Places:

Bobby Kerr Park, Hamilton, Ontario

Olympic record:

Member of Canadian track and field team, 1904, St. Louis

Gold medal, track and field, 200-metre, 1908, London

Bronze medal, track and field, 100-metre, 1908, London

Dave King

Places:

Dave King Park, Saskatoon, Saskatchewan

Olympic record:

4th place, head coach, men's ice hockey, 1984, Los Angeles

4th place, head coach, men's ice hockey, 1988, Calgary

Silver medal, head coach, men's ice hockey, 1992, Barcelona, Spain

Cindy Klassen

Places:

Cindy Klassen Recreation Complex, Winnipeg, Manitoba

Cindy Klassen Way, Winnipeg, Manitoba

Olympic record:

Bronze medal, speed skating, 3,000-metre, 2002, Salt Lake City, United States

Gold medal (1,500-metre); 2 silver medals (1,000-metre; team pursuit); 2 bronze medals (3,000-metre; 5,000-metre), speed skating, 2006, Turin, Italy

Silken Laumann

Places:

Silken Laumann Drive, Newmarket, Ontario

Silken Laumann Way, Mississauga, Ontario

Olympic record:

Bronze medal, rowing, double sculls, 1984, Los Angeles

Bronze medal, rowing, single sculls, 1992, Barcelona

Silver medal, rowing, single sculls, 1996, Atlanta

John Lecky

Places:

John M.S. Lecky UBC Boathouse, Richmond, British Columbia

Olympic record:

Silver medal, rowing eights, 1960, Rome, Italy

Karen Magnussen

Places:

Karen Magnussen Recreation Centre, Vancouver, British
Columbia

Olympic record:

7th place, women's figure skating, 1968, Grenoble
Silver medal, women's figure skating, 1972, Sapporo, Japan

Elizabeth Manley

Places:

Elizabeth Manley Park, Ottawa, Ontario
Elizabeth Manley Arena, Ottawa, Ontario

Olympic record:

13th place, women's figure skating, 1984, Sarajevo, Yugoslavia
(now Bosnia-Herzegovina)
Silver medal, women's figure skating, 1988, Calgary

Percival Molson

Places:

Percival Molson Stadium, Montreal, Quebec

Olympic record:

Member of Canadian track and field team, 400-metre, 1904, St.
Louis, United States

Percy Norman

Places:

Percy Norman Aquatic Centre, Vancouver, British Columbia
The Percy Norman Olympic Curling Venue, Vancouver, British
Columbia

Olympic record:

Swimming coach, 1932, Los Angeles
Swimming coach, 1936, Berlin

Steve Omischl

Places:

The Steve Omischl Sports Field Complex, North Bay, Ontario

Olympic record:

11th overall, men's freestyle skiing, 2002, Salt Lake City

20th overall, men's freestyle skiing, 2006, Turin

8th overall, men's freestyle skiing, 2010, Vancouver, Canada

Kate Pace

Places:

Kate Pace Way, North Bay, Ontario

Olympic record:

19th place, women's downhill skiing, 1998, Nagano

Marita Payne

Places:

Marita Payne Park, Vaughan, Ontario

Olympic record:

Silver medal, track and field, 4x100-metre relay, 1984, Los Angeles

Silver medal, track and field, 4x400-metre relay, 1984, Los Angeles

Member of Canadian track and field team, 1988, Seoul, South
Korea

Pat Quinn

Places:

Pat Quinn Way, Hamilton, Ontario

Pat Quinn Parkdale Arena, Hamilton, Ontario

Olympic record:

Gold medal, coach, men's ice hockey, 2002, Salt Lake City

Mike Richards

Places:

Mike Richards Way, Kenora, Ontario

Olympic record:

Gold medal, men's ice hockey, 2010, Vancouver

Bobbie Rosenfeld

Places:

Bobbie Rosenfeld Park, Toronto, Ontario

Olympic record:

Silver medal, track and field, 4x100-metre, 1928, Amsterdam, Holland

Silver medal, track and field, 100-metre, 1928, Amsterdam

Sandra Schmirler

Places:

Sandra Schmirler Leisure Centre, Regina, Saskatchewan

Sandra Schmirler Way, Regina, Saskatchewan

Sandra Schmirler Olympic Gold Park, Biggar, Saskatchewan

Olympic record:

Gold medal, women's team curling, 1998, Nagano

Beckie Scott

Places:

Beckie Scott Nordic Centre, Invermere, British Columbia

Beckie Scott Loppet, Vermillion, Alberta

Olympic record:

Gold medal, cross-country skiing, combined pursuit, 2002, Salt Lake City

Silver medal, cross-country skiing, team sprint, 2006, Turin

Billy Sherring

Places:

Billy Sherring Park, Hamilton, Ontario

Olympic record:

Gold medal, marathon, 1906, Athens, Greece

Elvis Stojko

Places:

Elvis Stojko Arena, Richmond Hill, Ontario

Olympic record:

7th place, men's figure skating, 1992, Albertville

Silver medal, men's figure skating, 1994, Lillehammer
Silver medal, men's figure skating, 1998, Nagano

Jimmy Thompson

Places:

Jimmy Thompson Pool, Hamilton, Ontario

Olympic record:

Bronze medal, swimming, 4x200-metre freestyle, 1928, Amsterdam

George Vernot

Places:

George Vernot Park, Montreal, Quebec

Olympic record:

Silver medal, swimming, 1,500-metre freestyle, 1920, Antwerp, Belgium

Bronze medal, swimming, 400-metre freestyle, 1920, Antwerp

Harry Warren

Places:

Harry Warren Field, Vancouver, British Columbia

Olympic record:

Substitute, Canadian track and field team, 1928, Amsterdam

Percy Williams

Places:

Percy Williams Junior Public School, Toronto, Ontario

Olympic record:

Gold medal, track and field, 100-metre, 1928, Amsterdam
Gold medal, track and field, 200-metre, 1928, Amsterdam
Member of Canadian track and field team, 1932, Los Angeles

Harold Wright

Places:

Harold Wright Field, Vancouver, British Columbia

Olympic record:

Member of Canadian track and field team, 1932, Los Angeles

Appendix B

Halls of Fame

Many sports figures honoured with Canadian place names have been inducted into a hall of fame. This list shows which hall(s) of fame they belong to, the year they were inducted, and the Canadian places named for them.

Bob Abate
Places:
    Bob Abate Community Recreation Centre, Toronto, Ontario
Inducted:
    Canadian Sports Hall of Fame, 1976

Ned Andreoni
Places:
    The Ned Andreoni Gymnasium, Moose Jaw, Saskatchewan
Inducted:
    Saskatchewan Baseball Hall of Fame, 2010

Syl Apps
Places:
    Syl Apps Youth Centre, Oakville, Ontario
    Syl Apps Community Centre, Paris, Ontario
    Syl and Molly Apps Research Centre, Kingston, Ontario
Inducted:
    Hockey Hall of Fame, 1961

Susan Auch

Places:

Susan Auch Park, Winnipeg, Manitoba

Susan Auch Speed Skating Oval, Winnipeg, Manitoba

Inducted:

Manitoba Sports Hall of Fame, 2003

Harry Bailey

Places:

Harry Bailey Aquatic Centre, Saskatoon, Saskatchewan

Inducted:

Saskatchewan Sports Hall of Fame, 1973

Nat Bailey

Places:

Nat Bailey Stadium, Vancouver, British Columbia

The Nat Bailey Farmer's Market, Vancouver, British Columbia

Inducted:

British Columbia Sports Hall of Fame, 2003

Emery Barnes

Places:

Emery Barnes Park, Vancouver, British Columbia

Inducted:

Oregon State Sports Hall of Fame, 1986

Jean Béliveau

Places:

Colisée Jean-Béliveau, Longueuil, Quebec

Pavillon Jean-Béliveau, Victoriaville, Quebec

Inducted:

Hockey Hall of Fame, 1972

Marilyn Bell

Places:

Marilyn Bell Park, Toronto, Ontario

Inducted:
> Canadian Sports Hall of Fame, 1958
> Canadian Swimming Hall of Fame, 1993

Max Bell

Places:
> Max Bell Aquatic Centre, University of Lethbridge, Lethbridge, Alberta
> Max Bell Arena, Calgary, Alberta

Inducted:
> Canadian Horse Racing Hall of Fame, 1977

Hilton Belyea

Places:
> Hilton Belyea Arena, Saint John, New Brunswick

Inducted:
> New Brunswick Sports Hall of Fame, 1971

Leo Boivin

Places:
> Leo Boivin Community Centre, Prescott, Ontario

Inducted:
> Hockey Hall of Fame, 1986

Ray Bourque

Places:
> Aréna Raymond-Bourque, Saint-Laurent, Quebec

Inducted:
> Hockey Hall of Fame, 2004

Johnny Bright

Places:
> Johnny Bright Sports Park, Edmonton, Alberta
> Johnny Bright Stadium, Edmonton, Alberta
> Johnny Bright School, Edmonton, Alberta

Inducted:
> Canadian Football Hall of Fame, 1970

Tom Brook

Places:

Tom Brook Athletic Park, Calgary, Alberta

Inducted:

Canadian Football Hall of Fame, 1975

Kurt Browning

Places:

Kurt Browning Arena, Caroline, Alberta

Inducted:

World Figure Skating Hall of Fame, 2006

Jack Couch

Places:

Jack Couch Stadium, Kitchener, Ontario

Inducted:

Waterloo County Hall of Fame, circa 1970

Yvan Cournoyer

Places:

Olympia Yvan-Cournoyer, Drummondville, Quebec

Inducted:

Hockey Hall of Fame, 1982

Eric Coy

Places:

Eric Coy Arena, Winnipeg, Manitoba

Eric Coy Neighbourhood, Winnipeg, Manitoba

Inducted:

Canadian Track and Field Hall of Fame, 1963

Canadian Sports Hall of Fame, 1971

Manitoba Sports Hall of Fame, 1980

Buddy Daye

Places:

Buddy Daye Street, Halifax, Nova Scotia

Inducted:

Nova Scotia Sports Hall of Fame, 1981 (boxing)

Jack Diamond

Places:

Jack and Sadie Diamond University Centre, Simon Fraser
University, Vancouver, British Columbia

Jack and Sadie Diamond Building, Simon Fraser University,
Vancouver, British Columbia

Inducted:

Canadian Horse Racing Hall of Fame, 1977

Marcel Dionne

Places:

Centre Marcel Dionne, Drummondville, Quebec

Inducted:

Hockey Hall of Fame, 1992

Rocky DiPietro

Places:

Rocky DiPietro Field, Sault Ste. Marie, Ontario

Inducted:

Canadian Football Hall of Fame, 1997

Clarence Downey

Places:

Clarence Downey Speed Skating Oval, Saskatoon, Saskatchewan

Inducted:

Saskatchewan Sports Hall of Fame, 1967

Saskatoon Sports Hall of Fame, 1986

Bill Durnan

Places:

Aréna Bill Durnan, Montreal, Quebec

Inducted:

Hockey Hall of Fame 1964

Rod Gilbert

Places:

Aréna Rodrigue-Gilbert, Montreal, Quebec

Inducted:

Hockey Hall of Fame, 1982

Foster Hewitt

Places:

The Foster Hewitt Media Gondola, Toronto, Ontario

Inducted:

Hockey Hall of Fame, Builder Category, 1965

Sue Holloway

Places:

Sue Holloway Fitness Park, Ottawa, Ontario

Inducted:

Canadian Olympic Hall of Fame, 1986

Charmaine Hooper

Places:

Charmaine Hooper Fields, Ottawa, Ontario

Inducted:

United Soccer League Hall of Fame, 2002

Tim Horton

Places:

The Tim Horton Events Centre, Cochrane, Ontario

Inducted:

Hockey Hall of Fame, 1977

Fergie Jenkins

Places:

Fergie Jenkins Parkway, Chatham, Ontario

Fergie Jenkins Park, Chatham, Ontario

Inducted:

Baseball Hall of Fame, 1991 (first Canadian)

David Johnston

Places:

The David Johnston Research and Technology Park, Waterloo, Ontario

Inducted:

Harvard University Athletic Hall of Fame, 1988

Teeder Kennedy

Places:

Teeder Kennedy Youth Arena, Port Colborne, Ontario

Inducted:

Hockey Hall of Fame, 1966

Dave Keon

Places:

Aréna Dave Keon, Rouyn-Noranda, Quebec

Inducted:

Hockey Hall of Fame, 1986

Brian Kilrea

Places:

Brian Kilrea Teaching Room, Children's Hospital, Ottawa, Ontario

Brian Kilrea Arena, Ottawa, Ontario

Inducted:

Hockey Hall of Fame, Builders category, 2003

Raymond Knight

Places:

Raymond Knight Stampede Grounds, Raymond, Alberta

Inducted:

Canadian Professional Rodeo Hall of Fame, 1982

Charlie Krupp

Places:

Charlie Krupp Stadium, Winnipeg, Manitoba

Inducted:

Manitoba Sports Hall of Fame (softball), 1989

Guy Lafleur

Places:

Aréna Guy-Lafleur, Thurso, Quebec

Inducted:

Hockey Hall of Fame, 1988

Norman "Pinky" Lewis

Places:

Norman Pinky Lewis Recreation Centre, Hamilton, Ontario

Inducted:

McMaster University Athletic Hall of Fame, 1989

Canadian Athletic Therapists Association Hall of Fame

Harry Lumley

Places:

Harry Lumley Bayshore Community Centre, Owen Sound, Ontario

Inducted:

Hockey Hall of Fame, 1980

Ken MacLeod

Places:

The Honourable Ken MacLeod Field, Kiwanis Park, Regina,
Saskatchewan

Inducted:

Regina Sports Hall of Fame, 2010

Duncan McGeachy

Places:

McGeachy Fields, St. Stephen's High School, St. Stephen, New
Brunswick

Inducted:

New Brunswick Sports Hall of Fame, 2011

Mark Messier

Places:

Mark Messier Trail, Edmonton, Alberta

Mark Messier Rink, St. Albert, Alberta

Inducted:

Hockey Hall of Fame, 2007

Greg Moore

Places:

Greg Moore Youth Centre, Maple Ridge, British Columbia

Inducted:

Canadian Motorsport Hall of Fame, 2000

Howie Morenz

Places:

Aréna Howie-Morenz, Montreal, Quebec

Inducted:

Hockey Hall of Fame, 1945

Bill Mosienko

Places:

Billy Mosienko Arena, Winnipeg, Manitoba

Inducted:

Hockey Hall of Fame, 1965

Manitoba Sports Hall of Fame, 1980

Percy Norman

Places:

Percy Norman Aquatic Centre, Vancouver, British Columbia

The Percy Norman Olympic Curling Venue, Vancouver, British Columbia

Inducted:

British Columbia Sports Hall of Fame

Willie O'Ree

Places:

The Willie O'Ree Place, Fredericton, New Brunswick

New Brunswick Sports Hall of Fame, 1984

Inducted:

Breitbard Hall of Fame (honours San Diego athletes), 2008

Bobby Orr

Places:

Bobby Orr Community Centre Museum, Parry Sound, Ontario
Bobby Orr Hall of Fame, Parry Sound, Ontario
Bobby Orr Public School, Oshawa, Ontario

Inducted:

Hockey Hall of Fame, 1979

Marita Payne

Places:

Marita Payne Park, Vaughan, Ontario

Inducted:

Florida State University Sports Hall of Fame, 1991

Jacques Plante

Places:

Aréna Jacques-Plante, Shawinigan, Quebec

Inducted:

Hockey Hall of Fame, 1978

Jack Purcell

Places:

Jack Purcell Park, Ottawa, Ontario
Jack Purcell Lane, Ottawa, Ontario
Jack Purcell Community Centre, Ottawa, Ontario

Inducted:

Canadian Sports Hall of Fame, 1955

Maurice "Rocket" Richard

Places:

Aréna Maurice-Richard, Montreal, Quebec.

Inducted:

Hockey Hall of Fame, 1961

Bobbie Rosenfeld

Places:

Bobbie Rosenfeld Park, Toronto, Ontario

Inducted:

Canadian Sports Hall of Fame, 1955

Fred Salvador

Places:

Fred Salvador Field, Timmins, Ontario

Inducted:

Canadian Arm Wrestling Federation Hall of Fame, 2002

Terry Sawchuk

Places:

Terry Sawchuk Memorial Park, Winnipeg, Manitoba

Terry Sawchuk Arena, Winnipeg, Manitoba

Inducted:

Manitoba Sports Hall of Fame, 1982

Hockey Hall of Fame, 1971

Dannie Seaman

Places:

Dannie Seaman Sports Field, Liverpool, Nova Scotia

Inducted:

Nova Scotia Sports Hall of Fame, 1980

Babe Siebert

Places:

Babe Siebert Memorial Arena, Zurich, Ontario

Inducted:

Hockey Hall of Fame, 1964

E.P. Taylor

Places:

E.P. Taylor Place, Toronto, Ontario

E.P. Taylor Research Library and Archives, Toronto, Ontario

Inducted:

Canadian Sports Hall of Fame, 1976

Canadian Horse Racing Hall of Fame, 1976

George Vernot

Places:

George Vernot Park, Montreal, Quebec

Inducted:

McGill Sports Hall of Fame, 1998

Gilles Villeneuve

Places:

Circuit Gilles Villeneuve, Montreal, Quebec

Gilles Villeneuve Park, Berthierville, Quebec

Inducted:

Canadian Motorsports Hall of Fame, 1993

Henry Viney

Places:

Henry Viney Arena, Calgary, Alberta

Inducted:

Alberta Sports Hall of Fame, 1983

Harry Warren

Places:

Harry Warren Field, Vancouver, British Columbia

Inducted:

British Columbia Sports Hall of Fame, 1990

University of British Columbia Sports Hall of Fame, 1993

Jozo Weider

Places:

Jozo Weider Boulevard, Collingwood, Ontario

Inducted:

Canadian Ski Hall of Fame, 1983

Ed Whalen

Places:

The Ed Whalen Broadcast Gondola, Scotiabank Saddledome,
Calgary, Alberta

Ed Whalen Ice Rink, Southland Leisure Centre, Calgary, Alberta

Inducted:

Slam! Wrestling Canadian Hall of Fame, 1998

Sade and Wilda Widmeyer

Places:

The Sade and Wilda Widmeyer Baseball Diamond, Fergus, Ontario

Inducted:

Canadian Amateur Softball Hall of Fame in Ottawa, 1997

Alan Wilson

Places:

Alan Wilson Park, Duncan, British Columbia

Alan Wilson Grove, Duncan, British Columbia

Inducted:

Canadian Football Hall of Fame, 1997

BC Lions Hall of Fame, 1997

Harold Wright

Places:

Harold Wright Field, Vancouver, British Columbia

Inducted:

Canadian Amateur Sports Hall of Fame, 1987

Andy Zwack

Places:

Andy Zwack Baseball Diamond, Saskatoon, Saskatchewan

Inducted:

Saskatchewan Sports Hall of Fame, 1993

Index